Finally, the inspiring story of St. Faustina for young readers! Far from a mere gathering of historic details, this is an engaging and readable biography. In her personal, conversational style, Donna-Marie Cooper O'Boyle is simply telling the story of one of her favorite saints. It's a compelling story and, as it unfolds, she invites her readers to think about their own relationship with Christ, offering them practical ways to model their lives on Faustina's. Though geared primarily for young people, this is perhaps the fullest and richest biography of St. Faustina and will be a great blessing for young and old alike.

— **Vinny Flynn,** author of *7 Secrets of Divine Mercy*

I can't think of a more timely or necessary book for our times than Donna-Marie Cooper O'Boyle's wonderful biography, *Diary of a Future Saint.* Devotion to the Divine Mercy — the simple message that God's mercy is greater than our sins — is absolutely essential to navigating through the dark, dangerous, and confusing times in which we live. This biography reads like an exciting novel, yet it is completely orthodox, drawing heavily from the saint's famous *Diary,* as well as from Sacred Scripture and the *Catechism.* Not only is Donna-Marie's book an invaluable resource for anyone interested in the life of the humble Polish nun, but it also provides meditations, prayers, and actions that serve to immerse the reader in God's infinite love and mercy. I highly recommend it.

— **Anthony DeStefano,** author of
A Travel Guide to Heaven,
Ten Prayers God Always Says Yes To,
and *Our Lady's Wardrobe*

Donna-Marie Cooper O'Boyle has written a vivid and penetrating biography of this luminous saint. *Diary of a Future Saint* pulls back the curtain on this remarkable woman to discover the splendor of her humble life. Beautiful details of her childhood, entry into religious life, and personal encounters with Jesus and Mary are presented here that prepared her to become the apostle of Divine Mercy. This biographical gem, which is both timely and timeless, shows how simple, childlike faith — like that of St. Faustina — reveal both the depth of God's love for us and our ability to participate deeply in His life.

> — **Deacon Harold Burke-Sivers,** author of *Our Life of Service: The Handbook for Catholic Deacons*

Maureen and I thoroughly enjoyed reading *Diary of a Future Saint*. We deeply appreciate the short chapters and suggestions presented to the reader. From the moment we picked up this wonderful biography, it was like any good work — once one begins reading, one cannot put the book down, but look forward to what was coming next. Being involved with the work of Divine Mercy at the National Shrine of The Divine Mercy and St. Faustina's cause for beatification and now sainthood, we highly encourage and recommend this book — it's worth every word in it.

> — **Deacon Bob and Maureen Digan;** *Maureen was the miracle for Sr. Faustina's beatification.*

Diary of a Future Saint is an exceedingly enjoyable book to read. You learn some fascinating details about Faustina's life — at home, in the big city, in the convent — and you realize that the life of a saint can be quite a bumpy ride. We get to see her very human responses to the trials and tribulations the Lord allowed her to go through. But, you also get a good dose of the weird, the freaky, and the strange that is uniquely Catholic. Visions of Jesus, Mary, angels, and saints. Visits from souls of the dead in Purgatory and from souls of people who are about to die. Travels into Purgatory and hell. Awesome stuff! I highly recommend this book not only for the younger generation, but for anyone of any age who is interested in learning more about this fascinating saint, and more about the life beyond.

— **John Martignoni,** EWTN TV and radio host;
founder/president, Bible Christian Society

Saint Faustina was canonized as the first Saint of the new millennium: like the message Christ gave her to promote, and like the lives of all our Saints, she looks to the future, not the past, with the hope of Mercy and holiness. Donna-Marie Cooper O'Boyle's biography beautifully presents Faustina's life, message, and struggles for our young people with admirable clarity to help inspire them to foster a deep relationship with Jesus and look to the future with confidence, trusting in His Divine Mercy.

— **Father John S. Hogan, OCDS,** author;
co-host of EWTN's *Forgotten Heritage*

Young children are capable of great holiness. This book will help them get there!

— **Ralph Martin, S.T.D.**, director of Graduate Theology Programs in the New Evangelization, Sacred Heart Major Seminary, Archdiocese of Detroit

In *Diary of a Future Saint*, Donna-Marie Cooper O'Boyle captures the simple spirituality of St. Faustina. God works through the seemingly insignificant, making them exceptional saints by revealing to them the greatest messages from Heaven. The least credible in the eyes of the world sometimes possess tremendous knowledge, requiring us to humbly accept that it is the message, not the messenger, we must find reliable. This lesson, as with the three shepherd children of Fatima and St. Bernadette of Lourdes, is the disposition of our hearts; it prepares our minds so we can understand what God is telling us. This book is a must read for those, who, in these difficult times, need to fully comprehend who we are to become if we expect God to interact in us.

— **David M. Carollo,** executive director, World Apostolate of Fatima, USA/Our Lady's Blue Army

"And while I was sitting there, the sisters came along and were astounded to find me sitting on the table, and each one had her say. One said that I was a loafer and another, "What an eccentric!" I was a postulant at the time. Others said, "What kind of sister will she make?" Still, I could not get down because sister had ordered me to sit there by virtue of obedience until she told me to get down. Truly, God alone knows how many acts of self-denial it took. I thought I'd die of shame" (*Diary*, 151).

Diary of a Future Saint

of a

Future Saint

FAUSTINA'S
INCREDIBLE JOURNEY

Donna-Marie Cooper O'Boyle

Illustrated by Michael Ornido

© 2023 Donna-Marie Cooper O'Boyle. All rights reserved.

Available from:
Marian Helpers Center
Stockbridge, MA 01263

Prayerline: 1-800-804-3823
Orderline: 1-800-462-7426

Websites:
TheDivineMercy.org
ShopMercy.org

Library of Congress Control Number: 2023939164
ISBN: 978-1-59614-586-3

Imprimi Potest:
Very Rev. Chris Alar, MIC
Provincial Superior
The Blessed Virgin Mary, Mother of Mercy Province
Divine Mercy Sunday
April 16, 2023

Nihil Obstat:
Robert A. Stackpole, STD
Censor Deputatus
April 16, 2023

Scripture texts in this work are from the New Revised Standard Version Bible: Catholic Edition, copyright © 1989, 1993 the Division of Christian Education of the National Council of the Churches of Christ in the United States of America. Used by permission. All rights reserved. Excerpts from the English translation of the *Catechism of the Catholic Church* for use in the United States of America Copyright © 1994, United States Catholic Conference, Inc. — Libreria Editrice Vaticana. Used with Permission. English translation of the *Catechism of the Catholic Church*: Modifications from the Editio Typica copyright © 1997, United States Conference of Catholic Bishops — Libreria Editrice Vaticana.

I dedicate this book lovingly to my children:
Justin, Chaldea, Jessica, Joseph, and Mary-Catherine,
and to my grandchildren: Shepherd and Leo.
I also dedicate this book to Saint Faustina,
my Sister in Christ,
and to Our Lady of Czestochowa.

Table of Contents

On August 25, 1905, at eight in the morning,
a very precious "spark" came into the world.

1

A Saint-in-the-Making Is Born

The relentless pounding against the kitchen window captured the young novice's attention. She could not recall having ever heard the rain quite so fierce. It seemed like it could break the window! The Sister dropped her dish towel on the kitchen counter and walked to the window, her long black religious habit gently flowed and swished lightly with each of her quick steps. She reached for the white cotton curtain and quickly pulled it back to peer outside. The pouring rain beat down with a vengeance, splashing all over. Squinting hard through the wet window pane, Sister could hardly make out the yonder garden or even the nearby gate through the sheets of rain. Being on gate duty, she wondered for a minute how many beggars would come to the convent's gate on such a stormy day. *Would any dare venture out on a day like today?*

It really didn't matter how many would visit. She was simply curious because of the inclement weather. It was the kind of cold rain that chilled you right to the bone. Best to stay inside today. Then again, if you are hungry and have no food, you might have to come out. This young nun knew in her heart that Jesus desired for her to serve each person who came to the gate with an abundance of love — not just with food. The love might have been even more important than the gifts of food. After all, everyone needs food for the body, but also for the heart and soul. And folks who are experiencing rough times can surely benefit from a dose of love. Sister was always eager to help each and every visitor. Many a time, she also doled out a measure of spiritual advice too.

The ringing bell

Sister went back to her dirty pots and pans and began to silently pray as she scrubbed away, when suddenly, the startling ringing of the bell at the gate snapped her out of her quiet contemplation. The ringing became persistent, as the young nun grabbed her shawl, quickly wrapped it around her shoulders, and hurriedly made her way to answer the gate.

Upon arriving at the gate, the sister found a young man, standing in the pouring rain, soaked to the skin. He looked emaciated and apparently, hungry. Sister couldn't help but notice that the man lacked shoes and socks and had nothing covering his head. His clothes were in shreds. She motioned to him that she would return with something for him to eat as she hurried again — this time, back inside.

After a couple of moments of quandary because she could not find anything she thought suitable to offer, the young nun decided to reheat some soup she found in the refrigerator. After ladling it into a bowl, to give it a bit more substance, she grabbed a piece of bread and crumbled it over the top of the soup — she wanted to help nourish that poverty-stricken man. Sister then rushed back outside.

The poor man ate the gift of soup at the gate in the pouring rain. He seemed extremely satisfied as he finished every last drop and crumb of bread. Sister took the empty bowl from his cold wet hands and at once, she realized that the man was actually Jesus Christ Himself!

What an incredible miracle! Can you even imagine this?

As soon as Sister realized exactly WHO the man was, the holy visitor vanished completely from her sight! There was just so much for her to take in. Her heart was on fire with emotion. She went inside to reflect upon what just occurred.

Immediately, she heard these words, **"My daughter, the blessings of the poor who bless Me as they leave this gate have reached My ears. And your compassion, within the bounds of obedience, has pleased Me, and this is why I came down from My throne — to taste the fruits of your mercy."**[1]

The nun spoke to Jesus. "O my Jesus, now everything is clear to me, and I understand all that has just happened." Sister reflected, "I somehow felt and asked myself what sort of a poor man is this who radiates such modesty. From that moment on, there was stirred up in my heart an even purer love toward the poor and the needy."

As she pondered it all deeply, she felt incredibly happy and began to understand more and more about what it means to be merciful. Such a lowly task was given her to in answering the gate. But God rewarded her with the gift of Himself. This sister actually fed Jesus!

"Oh, how happy I am that my superiors have given me such a task! I understand that mercy is manifold; one can do good always and everywhere and at all times."

She realized, "An ardent love of God sees all around itself constant opportunities to share itself through deed, word, and prayer. Now I understand the words which You spoke to me, O Lord, some time ago."[2]

She knew in her heart that Jesus' instructions to all of us in Scripture, "Truly I tell you, just as you did it to one of the least of these who are members of my family, you did it to me" (Mt 25:40) were being realized in that moment.

But let's not get too far ahead of ourselves! We will later learn how and why this young nun, who happens to be Sr. Maria Faustina Kowalska, was called to the convent gate in the first place. Regardless of how and why, we first need to go back to the very beginning so we can learn and understand more.

Let's step back about 20 years before the miraculous ringing of that bell.

A spark enters the world

One morning, in the small hamlet of Głogowiec, one could clearly see the morning droplets of dew glistening across the meadow, as a foggy mist rose up from the damp ground and swiftly rolled away into the distant hills. The sun made his face known and began to warm the land. A hot summer day promised to be on tap in that particular region of Poland.

The songbirds seemed perfectly content, albeit a bit excited and as busy as ever, flying this way and that — every so often, perching on nearby branches, or even on the fence posts to then proudly stick out their feathered bellies and sing their morning melodies. Could they be trying to announce something special?

We shall see.

A swarm of barn swallows occasionally flew in and out of the barn's rafters. The roosters had finished their morning crowing, and along with the hens, were now scratching at bugs in the dirt at the Kowalska's small family farm. The family's many cows were already out in the pasture after happily being fed and relieved to have been milked, when the young Kowalska children Josephine and Eve slowly opened their glassy eyes to greet a new day.

Streams of bright yellow sunlight pierced through the plain muslin curtains which were pulled across the windows in their tiny two-room limestone home. And the sun's rays danced across the children's pillows. It was time to get up! However, breakfast time in the Kowalska household would be a bit different this morning. Mama wouldn't be cooking. Thankfully, though, she had already baked some of her delicious bread the other day. She had an inkling it would be a good idea to bake some extra loaves. After all, she was expecting a visitor! So, along with fresh chicken eggs and their cow's raw milk, even though Mama couldn't cook this morning, the Kowalska's breakfast would still be just about as delightful as ever!

Even if Papa didn't have time to cook the eggs, on such a morning as this one, the children would feast on fresh bread and milk. Nevertheless, it was a most special day to be sure. One of *the* most special days ever! That is because their mother Marianna had just given birth! Josephine and Eve would soon meet their baby sister. This peasant Polish family had been exceedingly eager for this very day to arrive. Marianna's eagerness was actually a perfect blend of excitement with a bit of trepidation because of her previous childbirths, which were still fresh on her mind. A mother never forgets.

On August 25, 1905, at eight in the morning, a very precious "spark" came into the world. The Catholic couple decided to name their baby girl Helena. She would later be called Jesus' "Secretary of Divine Mercy," and even much later, St. Pope John Paul II would speak about this "spark"[3] and also how Helena was "a gift of God for our time."[4] We will learn more about this later on.

For right now, we speak of that very moment when Marianna knew not a thing about what the future would bring for her newborn baby, born at the dawn of the twentieth century. All she could possibly do, was to lovingly gaze upon her new baby daughter, now snuggled warm and cozy against her body. This happy mother smiled like she had never smiled before as she held her baby tight. Marianna was most grateful for her third child.

God had been good to their family. Marianna and her husband Stanislaus together gave great praise to God for the gift and blessing of another child and they offered to Him an abundance of thanks for an easy delivery for Marianna.

Just two days later, Helena was baptized by Fr. Joseph Chodynski in St. Casimir Church in Świnice Warckie at a beautiful baptismal font that is still standing today at the time of this writing. At the juncture of Helena's birth and baptism, a cholera plague had stricken the area. People had been warned to not visit the area if it was not an emergency. It's possible, that Helena's parents wanted to have their baby baptized quickly after her birth to ensure her entrance into Heaven in case she became afflicted with cholera.

When Helena Kowalska entered the world, times were very restless in Poland. In Warsaw, only 30 miles away from Świnice, Martial law had been declared. This was not a good thing. Russian became the official language in the Polish schools as Russian teachers steadily replaced the Polish. Students and teachers went on strikes to oppose the Russification of their educational system.

There were many kinds of strikes and demonstrations, and also armed struggles between peasants and workers against the restrictive government autocratic rule. The demonstrators demanded improved economic and living conditions, as well as political freedoms for the workers.

In the year 1905 when Helena was born, Poland was on the verge of a civil war, or revolution against the Russian Empire. People lived in fear and clung to their faith a bit tighter. The atmosphere was tense, to say the least.

Family life

As the years rolled along, God blessed the Kowalska family with seven more children. They all grew up together, lovingly cramped in their small abode on the family farm in Głogowiec, which was near Łęczyca, in the parish of Świnice Warckie.

Father Stanislaus supported his family with his farming abilities and also his carpentry skills. Still, the family did not own much of anything, with the exception of their simple limestone thatched roof home and limestone farm buildings built by Stanislaus, and situated on a few acres he bought from the Olejniczak family.

Limestone is an ancient and long lasting material deposit which has been used by architects for thousands of years. However, as Stanislaus built his family's home, he probably didn't know that the same material he used to build his house was also used for building the Pyramids of Giza.

That was surely the farthest from his mind as he set to work with his simple tools to provide for his family. He had no idea about how large his family would grow. However, that did not matter. His faith in God prodded him to trust that the Lord of all would provide for whatever size family he would have. And he knew he should always strive his best to follow God's commands.

This Polish peasant toiled away at the limestone, praying interiorly, and he fashioned a fine sturdy one-story, two-room house which contained a hall way in between them and a kitchen on the right. One room was larger and served as the bedroom and living area. Stanislaus also built the farm buildings out of limestone which was inexpensive and a characteristic style of that area and era. He could easily get his limestone from a nearby quarry in Rozniatow.

As the family grew larger, the house might have seemed a bit smaller — especially during the winter time when Stanislaus took his carpentry work and tools inside. Marianna's daily bread baking always made the family home smell absolutely delightful and inviting. She never once read a recipe, but Marianna had learned through practice to be a master baker. It's a good thing she acquired this ability since she did not know how to read.

Sacramentals, teachings, and prayer traditions

Though the family lived in meager quarters and did not own much, they did have a few special religious items which adorned their humble abode. Pictures of Jesus and Mary hung on the wall of the main living area of their home. A small homemade family altar on which stood a metal crucifix that Stanislaus brought home from a pilgrimage he made to Czestochowa was a particular focal point for their family prayer. It was before that simple crucifix that Helena, the future St. Faustina, would often kneel to pray.

Helena was also influenced and inspired by a daily prayer tradition of her father which remained etched upon her heart all throughout her life. Every morning, as far back as Helena could remember, while everyone else in the family was asleep, and even before the roosters began to crow, Stanislaus rose from bed to greet the new day with prayer.

It wasn't just any prayer. It wasn't even a quiet prayer. Stanislaus fervently sang *The Little Office of the Immaculate Conception*. During Lent, he sang the penitential Psalms. In a tiny house, there was no escaping Stanislaus's outbursts of song coming from the very depths of his being. It's possible the children pulled their pillows over their ears, but nonetheless, their father's strong devotion was also a teaching about dedication to prayer.

It didn't matter to Stanislaus that his wife Marianna might have desperately wanted to get a bit more sleep before rising for the day, or that the children were still sound asleep. Stanislaus sang his heart out! He was fully dedicated to praising God and honoring the Mother of God in song. If his family protested, he told them that his first duty — was to serve God and after that his family.

The Kowalska family was a faithful one. Marianna was thankful for her husband's faith in God. "One of the traits she liked about Stanislaus was that 'the Faith was very important to him,'" she said. Though Marianna was illiterate, she still taught essential faith lessons to her children. She said, "Though I could not read or write, I taught my daughters and sons the truths of the Gospel, taking care that they not only knew the precept of love of neighbor, but, primarily, that they observed it."[5]

These prayerful parents worked together to instill a firm and faithful Catholic foundation in their family. Marianna said of her husband, "Stanislaus was an example to them of daily prayer and obligatory participation in Sunday Mass."

Speaking of Sunday Mass, because the family was poor, they owned only one church dress to be shared among the three girls: Josephine, Eve, and Helena. That meant the girls had to take turns going to Sunday Mass. When Helena couldn't go to Mass, she spent the time in quiet prayer, uniting her heart and soul to the Mass and asked for Spiritual Communion from Jesus since she could not receive Sacramentally at Mass.

We shall soon see that in time, Helena became a soul of prayer. God had His eye on her and was calling her to a special life of prayer. It was up to Helena to decide what she would do. Would she listen to God's whispers to her heart and soul? Was there any other way? We will get to that in Chapter Two! First, let's think about a few things.

Something to think about

Take a few minutes to think about the poverty of Helena's family and the simplicity of their lives. Remember, there was only one church dress between three daughters, and the entire family lived in a two-room house. Think of all of your own belongings. Could you be happy with fewer material things? Could you try to put less emphasis on your belongings and focus on important things such as family relationships and your faith life? Try your best to spend more time in prayer and with people and less time with things.

Take a few minutes to think about St. Faustina's encounter with Jesus in the disguise of a beggar at the very beginning of this chapter. What would you do if it happened to you? Also, can you try to prayerfully live your life being more aware of Jesus living within others? Can you try to be kinder to others? Think of a few ways you can be kind, even to someone who is not nice to you. How about smiling at them?

What do you think about Helena's father Stanislaus singing his prayers loudly every morning? Take a moment to think about how his example of dedication to prayer has influenced his family.

With regard to serving beggars at the gate, Faustina commented on her work and had said, "Oh, how happy I am that my superiors have given me such a task! I understand that mercy is manifold; one can do good always and everywhere and at all times." What do you think about your chores and tasks? Can you try not to complain and do them with love to please God and your family?

Pray

Dear Jesus and Mary, please guide me. Jesus, I trust in You! Help me to recognize You in others and serve You with love. Dear St. Faustina, please pray for me.

A Merciful Action

Endeavor to do a kind deed for a complete stranger sometime soon.

Helena loved to care for their cows. Since she was very mature for her age, she often brought the cows out to pasture and took them back to the barn before sunset.

2

God Has Big Plans for a Farm Girl

Helena grew to be a happy child. Her parents were pleased that she was exceptionally obedient and that she unfailingly desired to help around the household and the farm. If her parents could have a favorite child, she was the one! Of course, her parents loved all of their other children. However, they were grateful to God for Helena's cheerful and positive disposition.

For the most part, Helena's daily life was predictable. It was a balance of prayer, play, and work. The entire family helped out with chores except for the babies. Helena loved to care for their cows. Since she was very mature for her age, she often brought the cows out to pasture and took them back to the barn before sunset.

At times, Helena carried a book with her to read as the cattle grazed. She leaned up against a rock or the fence post and stuck her nose in a favorite book. We might wonder if her father allowed her to take one of his books out of the house. Stanislaus owned a collection of books and was an avid reader, one of the two people in his region able to read.

At times, if others were in the fields with her, while the cattle were grazing, Helena told stories of the Lives of the Saints, pilgrims, hermits, and missionaries to them, having had memorized the stories from her father's books. She also told her younger siblings that she would enter a convent when she grew up and her siblings laughed because they didn't understand her.

Helena also paused from her reading and whatever else she was doing to thank God for the day, for her family, her life, and every good thing. Helena took time to pray. No one needed to remind her, for she was sensitive to God's promptings to her soul. That, and her mother's fine teachings, as well as her father's robust morning prayer ritual set a sturdy sacred foundation in Helena's life.

God touched her soul

In 1912, 7-year-old Helena attended a Vespers service at St. Casimir Church, the same church where she was baptized and where she worshiped with her family. During the service, while praying before the Blessed Sacrament, Helena's heart overflowed with God's deep and abiding peace. She experienced a profound mystical experience in which our Lord let her know that He called her to a more perfect and holy life.

Many years later, Helena wrote in her *Diary*, "[T]he love of God was imparted to me for the first time and filled my little heart; and the Lord gave me understanding of divine things."[6] We can only imagine the joy that filled her heart, knowing that the Lord of all was so close to her. Helena continued to be an optimistic and prayerful child.

After a while, Helena experienced a strange phenomenon. She was awakened certain nights by great flashes of light! She never knew when this would happen and was a bit surprised each time the mysterious light disturbed her slumber. However, she came to know that she should pray at those times and that her Guardian Angel had summoned her to wake up and pray!

Helena received her First Holy Communion from Fr. Roman Pawloski at the age of 9 in 1914. She made her first Confession at St. Casimir parish that same year. The same wooden confessional still stands today. When Helena received her Lord Jesus for the first time, she was quiet and kept to herself afterwards. She did not want to speak to anyone at that time since she was focused on the gift of receiving Jesus. Her elderly neighbor Mrs. Berezinska asked her why she was walking by herself. Helena simply replied, "I am not walking alone; I am with the Lord Jesus."[7]

Helena grew to be a very fine student at school. She learned much, but felt quite miserable when shunned by a couple of her female classmates, because they felt Helena was too poorly dressed for them to sit with her. Before long, Helena and the other older students left the school to make room for the younger children coming in. Helena only received three semesters of formal education.

A Soul of Mercy

Helena's middle name could have been "Mercy." After all, from early on, her heart was full of mercy for others, and most especially for the most in need. Helena stood out among others because of her precious awareness of the presence of God and His call to us to take care of His poor. Her family and her neighbors continually witnessed Helena's goodness and beautiful sense of mercy.

Even as a young girl, Helena was acutely aware of the needs of others around her. Not only that, she didn't just stand by, simply observing. No. She figured out ways to respond to the needs the best she could for her age. Oftentimes, poor people visited the area seeking mercy in the form of a piece of bread or a donation to help them through the day. Helena couldn't help but notice these people and sought ways to alleviate their hunger.

One time, the young compassionate *dziewczynka* came up with the idea of holding a lottery in order to raise money. Another time, she dressed up in her mother's old clothes to look like a beggar and went from door to door, begging money for the poor. She brought all of her collections to her parish priest to be used for the poor.

Life outside the farm

No longer in school, Helena begged her parents to allow her to work. She deeply desired to help support the family, knowing full well how her hard working father could not make ends meet. She was always good about doing her chores and helping in the home, however, she thought she should also put her hands to work outside the home to earn some money.

When Helena was 14 years old, her parents allowed her to become employed as a domestic servant for a family they knew who needed help. Helena prayed much, even during her work because she loved our Lord. After a year of this work, Helena returned home and boldly pleaded with her parents to allow her to join a convent.

These holy parents knew their daughter was a docile and holy soul, eager to please God. However, they would have no part of such pleadings and quickly put an end to her begging by telling their daughter flat out, the simple answer was, "No!" Helena's parents needed their daughter to help out in the household and farm and couldn't possibly afford the necessary dowry of money and clothing to enter the convent. At that time and place, no one could enter religious life without the provision of a dowry. The Kowalska family positively did not have a way in which to provide it.

Being an obedient soul, Helena listened well to her parents, though she might have shed a few quiet tears. She abided by their instructions and continued to do domestic work. Soon after, with their blessing, she courageously set out for the big city of Lodz, an industrial center and the second largest city in Poland. When Helena arrived in 1922, nearly one hundred thousand workers were employed there — 70 percent were factory workers. Still, there was an awful lot of unemployed, as well as poverty, and homelessness.

At that time, countless people were drawn to Lodz, desiring a profitable career, a fortune, and fine connections. Helena was not in search of such things. She simply followed her parents' instructions and pursued employment. Helena lived with her cousins.

Soon enough, in a city of over five hundred thousand inhabitants, Helena was providentially employed by three female members of the Third Order of St. Francis. Third Order members are often called tertiaries. Being spiritually minded themselves, the kind women were more than happy to allow 17-year-old Helena the time off for daily Mass, the Sacraments, and devotions. Helena also wanted time to visit the sick and dying.

An unexpected, but most wonderful additional benefit for Helena at such a pivotal time of her life was the easy access to the tertiaries' confessor, Fr. Wyzykowski! Helena was certainly helped spiritually by a holy priest. Helena sent most of her earnings home to help her family.

God was certainly watching over Helena and providing for her spiritual needs to be met. All Helena needed to do was to listen to God and move her own will to do the right things as she cooperated with God's grace. It's the same for you and me. We can all pray for God's grace and endeavor to follow God's holy will.

A little later, we'll learn about a most difficult predicament Helena found herself in with regard to listening to God's graces flowing into her heart and soul.

Helena thirsted for God

A year of work in Lodz passed and Helena returned home at 18 years old. After a life of deep longings for serving God, she mustered up her courage to beg her parents once again for their permission to enter religious life. She had hardly spoken before she sadly heard their same quick and stern reply.

"No!"

Yet, God continued to call to Helena. However, she felt extremely helpless. Many thoughts swirled around her brain. Was she imagining things? Did God really want her to be a religious sister? Why didn't her parents understand this? When her parents told Helena that they simply could not afford to provide a necessary dowry, Helena insisted that God would provide for it. Still, Stanislaus and Marianna wouldn't budge on their decision. They were poor, without even a *zloty* saved, and were unwilling to sell a needed family cow to provide for a dowry.

Helena felt perplexed because she knew with all her heart that God was calling her to a vocation to religious life, but she didn't know how she could possibly fulfill it. On top of that, she simply could not forget the experience she had when she was just 7 years old.

She later wrote in her *Diary*, "[F]or the first time, I heard God's voice in my soul; that is, an invitation to a more perfect life." Helena always did her best to stay prayerful and she strove to grow in holiness, but she also struggled. As she expressed, "I was not always obedient to the call of grace. I came across no one who would have explained these things to me."[8] As good as her well-meaning parents were in imparting the faith to her, Helena found no one who could truly understand the deep longings of her heart and the special call to grace. She felt very alone in this regard.

Helena shunned God

And now, at 18 years old, her thirst for Jesus seemed insatiable, but also most unobtainable. What could she do? Well, she tried to cope the best she could. Beyond question, her parents' flat out refusal crushed her spirit. Helena diverted her attention elsewhere as a form of survival mode — trying to protect her downcast heart.

This Polish farm lass, once without a dress to call her own, suddenly became interested in her appearance and involved herself with the glitter and bustle of city life. With the small portion of money she allowed for herself, she bought fashionable clothes, went to fairs and dances with her friends and sisters, who also lived and worked in Lodz, and she tried her hardest to drown out God's call to her heart — if that was at all possible.

Despite all of her efforts, Helena could not find one bit of happiness within any of these pastimes. She honestly admitted, "I turned myself over to the vain things of life, paying no attention to the call of grace, although my soul found no satisfaction in any of these things."

We can't exactly blame Helena for doing such things. She did not sin. However, she tried her best to keep herself distracted and she turned a deaf ear to God, believing it was completely futile for her to continue pursuing her dream and calling to enter the convent. No one was willing to help her. What else could she do?

Being involved in somewhat worldly things and not listening to God caused Helena to feel a deep turmoil in her heart and soul. How could she possibly escape God's call?

Later on, Helena expressed, "The incessant call of grace caused me much anguish; I tried, however, to stifle it with amusements. Interiorly, I shunned God, turning with all my heart to creatures. However, God's grace won out in my soul."[9]

We shall soon learn just how God won out in this young woman's soul.

Early works of mercy

Helena went back to work in Lodz as a domestic servant and also looked after children at the homes she worked. On a regular basis, Helena came across the unfortunate poor, sometimes behind tenement houses, behind places she worked. Not far from the tenement houses was a slum area where some of the poorest of the poor dwelled. Helena's heart was always pulled when seeing the struggles.

Helena made a most favorable impression on all who came to know her. She became known for her kindness, her smiles, and heartfelt giggles. She was someone you wanted as your friend.

Helena fasted regularly and even sang Eucharistic hymns to the children. The happy *dziewczyna* (girl) was also a great story teller, perhaps garnering this skill from her father, who also loved to tell stories. The children for whom she cared loved to gather around her for her gift of stories and fairy tales. Just as soon as Helena pulled up a stool — they were there! They sat at her feet, yearning for yet another story and they hung on every word.

Helena's employers had much praise for her and confidence in her, knowing their children were safe in her care. Some of her employers attended Mass and Confession more often because of Helena's fine example.

At one point, three Kowalska sisters worked in Lodz as domestic servants: Helena, Genowefa, and Natalia. They went to Mass at the Cathedral each Sunday and met afterwards to chat. They always kept in touch with one another and often worked in close proximities.

Helena's heart was certainly molded by her saintly parents and her Catholic faith. Even though, for a time, to a certain extent, she tried to tune out God, she still continued her devotions and also cared for the unfortunate. God had put a lot of love in her heart. She often looked around for someone she could help in some way.

It turned out that at one of her domestic jobs in Lodz, a lonely poverty stricken man, who was also sickly, lived in a storage closet located under the stairs. As soon as Helena learned about him, every chance she had, she brought food to the frail man, comforted him with her time and kind words, and even shared with him her love for God. After conversing with him, Helena believed he had to reconcile with God and she wanted to be of assistance.

Sacraments

During every visit, Helena talked to her new friend about God, hoping to stir the cold embers in his heart into a flame of love for God. At one point, Helena was certain she should quickly ask a priest to visit the man so he could receive the Sacraments of Confession and Holy Communion. Helena's sister Natalia was visiting Helena when the priest arrived to see the old man. Natalia noticed how frail the man was and how lovingly eager her older sister Helena was to take care of him — but also keen to assist him in getting to Heaven — the place we are all ultimately meant to live in Eternal happiness.

That day, the man willingly received the Sacraments from the priest. He died the following day. As much as we might be saddened to know that the man died, we can also be comforted, knowing that he was loved and had received important Sacraments from the Church that were most likely the precise *ticket* the man needed to get to Heaven![10]

Helena certainly guided this man to Heaven through her loving acts of mercy. It was no coincidence that God placed

Helena at that particular domestic job at that precise time when the old man was in most need.

We too, can ponder our own lives and pray that we can help others in need to get to Heaven through our own prayers and works of mercy.

The consequential dance

In the summer of 1924, on the outskirts of the city of Lodz, a county fair was enjoyed at Venice Park by the many people who came from near and far to try their hand at the variety of carnival games or to watch the clever magicians pull the wool over their eyes. Some simply strolled through the area among the chestnut trees and gazed off in the distance at the nearby Jaisen River while listening to the merriment. The orchestra played lively tunes, luring crowds of happy twirlers to the dance floor.

It was guaranteed to be a festive atmosphere and the Kowalska sisters and their friend Lucy Strzelecka decided to partake. Though, Helena's sisters had to persuade Helena to attend the dance because she was a bit hesitant. Eventually, Jeannie, Natalia, Helena, and their friend Lucy set off. They all looked very nice, dressing for the occasion. Helena wore a pleated pink frilly skirt. Her long hair was styled in a plait braid on the back of her head.

Shortly after their arrival, a few young men walked over and asked the young ladies for a dance. Helena was nervous and said she was not a very good dancer. Nevertheless, the young man smiled and Helena ventured out with him onto the dance floor, among the others who were already whirling and twirling and having great fun.

It should have been a happy time for Helena too. However, something rather dramatic happened that shook Helena to the core and caused her to experience intense turmoil. And it wasn't her lack of dance skills.

Only a moment into the dance and Helena stopped dancing. Someone had cut in. It was Jesus! Helena later explained, "While everybody was having a good time, my soul was experiencing deep torments."[11]

This specific summer evening became a remarkable and crucial moment of truth in Helena's life. It was one she never could have imagined in a million years! Yet, it unmistakably turned her world upside down and catapulted her off on an amazing holy journey!

Amazingly, Jesus showed up at the dance! Was Helena dreaming or was Jesus Christ really standing beside her? He appeared as if He had just come from the scourging at the pillar, covered in bloody wounds. He was visibly in excruciating pain, as well as stripped of His clothing.

Can we even imagine this? Yes, it was true. The timid dancer was not mistaken, though Helena was completely shocked. This miraculous moment occurred as soon as Helena began dancing with the young man! However, the holy drama didn't end there.

Jesus, then spoke up. **"How long shall I put up with you and how long will you keep putting Me off?"**[12]

Jesus remained

Helena was absolutely astounded to see and hear from Jesus Christ Himself. Just seconds before, to her observation, the charming music abruptly stopped playing and every single thing and person around her had disappeared from her sight — like it had been an illusion. Only Jesus remained — standing near and not mincing a word when He spoke. After He spoke, He vanished.

Helena, later wrote about the incredible occurrence in her *Diary*. She recalled, "[T]here remained Jesus and I. I took a seat by my dear sister pretending to have a headache in order to cover up what took place in my soul." Without delay, Helena left the dance. We will probably never know what the unsuspecting young man whose dance partner left in haste was thinking!

Where did she go? What was Helena thinking? She fled to the only place that made sense for her to go, especially after having that miraculous encounter with Jesus. Helena later recounted, "After a while I slipped out unnoticed, leaving my sister and all my companions behind and made my way to the Cathedral of Saint Stanislaus Kostka."[13]

Interestingly, St. Stanislaus Kostka, a patron saint of youth, seminarians, and young students also headed to religious life against his parents' wishes. When his parents refused to allow his entrance to religious life, Stanislaus secretly ran away from Vienna on August 10, 1567. He walked a very rugged journey, about 700 miles to Rome where he was accepted into the Jesuit order at 17 years of age.

Courage and Bewilderment

Back to Helena. Upon reaching the Cathedral at around twilight, Helena hurried inside. Totally oblivious to the people there, she threw herself down on the floor, and prostrated herself before Jesus in the Blessed Sacrament. She stretched out her arms as if in a cross. She could not forget that moment — perhaps a blend of courage and bewilderment, and she recorded it in her *Diary* sometime later.

She wrote, "I fell prostrate before the Blessed Sacrament and begged the Lord to be good enough to give me to understand what I should do next." We might ponder now the great courage Helena possessed to immediately flee the dance, blindly trusting that God would lead her to know exactly what to do. She pleaded and she trusted. Was this the beginning her great trust in God?

As soon as Helena pleaded with Jesus in the Blessed Sacrament, she heard these words: **"Go at once to Warsaw; you will enter a convent there."**[14]

Earlier, I mentioned that Helena wrote in her *Diary* how God would win out in her soul. Now we know that it was precisely when He captured her undivided attention, by dramatically appearing to her at the dance.

Incidentally, if you were to visit Venice Park in Lodz (now called Juliusz Slowacki Park), you would see flowers, religious items, ribbons, pictures, and more which St. Faustina devotees have left on and near a giant chestnut tree which is very close to the place Jesus appeared to Helena when she was dancing. A stone plaque is there as well to commemorate the place where 19-year-old Helena was visited by Jesus.

Back to our story. Helena just fled the dance and poured her heart out to Jesus in the Blessed Sacrament, received His instructions, and is about to take an unexpected holy journey she never could have envisioned. Before we get to that in our next chapter, first, let's ponder a few things.

 ## Something to think about

Take a few minutes to think about how God was calling to Helena's soul to strive to become holy. Helena wanted to listen to Him and felt inspired to enter religious life. When her parents wouldn't allow it, she turned away from God's graces and started to get involved with more worldly pastimes.

What do you think the danger is in this?

Could it be that if she wasn't careful and prayerful that she might turn completely away from God, through getting caught up with other distractions?

Could that happen to you?

Take a few moments to think about your own life and what you can do to be sure to listen more attentively to God.

Remember, Jesus had to shake Helena up with His dramatic appearance at the dance and ask her straight out, **"How long shall I put up with you and how long will you keep putting Me off?"**

While He most likely will not appear to us to ask us the same, could He be also speaking the same message to our hearts?

Think about Helena's desire to help people, like the poor old homeless man living under the stairs. Through her kindnesses to him and her prayers and encouragement, Helena was able to get the man interested in having a priest involved so that he could receive the Sacraments. As it turned out, it was right in the nick of time, just before he died.

Think about your own life and pray for opportunities to help others — even in your own family and neighborhood.

 ## Pray

Dear Jesus and Mary, please guide me. Jesus, I trust in You! Help me to have a caring heart like St. Faustina. Dear St. Faustina, please pray for me.

 ## A Merciful Action

Pray for an opportunity to sincerely and lovingly encourage someone and then act on it.

Whenever Helena had time off from her
domestic duties, she went into Warsaw to
knock on convent doors.

3

Knocking Until a Door Opens

It was July 1924, and Jesus distinctly told Helena to, "**Go at once to Warsaw.**" He also told her that she would enter a convent there. Even though, Helena had long yearned for religious life, and Jesus Himself directed her to go to Warsaw, Helena still worried about hurting her parents. She had been out of the family home and living on her own for some time now, working in Lodz and sending money home to her parents to help pay the bills. However, she knew full well her parents made it very clear to her that they did not want their daughter joining a convent, even though they were pious and had five other daughters and two sons.

In fact, at some point, a religious sister practically accused Helena's mother of being "stingy" with God. It was Sr. Wilczek. She decided to ask pious Marianna, who was blessed with many daughters, why it was that she was so opposed to allowing just one — just Helena from becoming a nun.

Marianna told her, "Because she was the best child, the dearest … and so obedient and hard-working, the most loving."[15] Of course, there was also the problem with the lack of a dowry, or money to purchase postulant clothes.

Helena, being so obedient, was frightened at what she was doing! She never defied her parents. She was definitely in a huge predicament. She was now opposing her parents' wishes by heading to Warsaw. Plus, they certainly relied on the financial help she sent home to them.

She eloped with Jesus!

Still, as much as this kind daughter loved and respected her parents, and as terrified as she was, she knew she needed to listen to Jesus. He had shaken her up with His clear and succinct words. These were undeniable words — specific words to lead her to a holy and more perfect life — a life Jesus had called her to, 12 years earlier at the young age of 7.

We can honestly say that this teen on the run planned to elope with Jesus!

Before going to Warsaw, Helena needed to go back home to the apartment where she lived to gather necessary things and to tie up any loose ends. Her plan was to set out for Warsaw in the morning. It wouldn't be easy because she had to first explain herself to her sister and her uncle. They might think she was crazy!

The morning came quickly after a restless night. Helena began to pack — just a few small things to bring with her to Warsaw. She tied them all up in a head scarf. All her clothing, with the exception of the one outfit she would wear, she gave to her uncle Michal Rapacki to send home to her parents and sisters. Helena traveled very light and believed that Jesus would provide for all of her needs.

Well, her uncle did think she was crazy. He even tried to stop her from leaving and heavily emphasized that if Helena left for Warsaw, she would cause great distress for her parents. As difficult as it was, Helena stood firm in her decision. She would listen to Jesus. Her uncle eventually realized he couldn't get in her way, and seeing how hard it was for Helena, he accompanied her to the train station.

A history-changing train journey

Helena knew what she had to do, but still, she boarded the train amid trepidation. She wiped away a few tears and found a seat. Her Uncle Michal could see her through the window as she walked through and sat down. Helena was sobbing. It broke his heart to see her cry so hard that she shook. He wanted to run in there to get her off the train. But there was no stopping that train. Off it went, chugging down the track, carrying his niece to the unknown.

Helena was now on her way. She'd get to Warsaw in about two hours and 20 minutes. We can imagine it was a very prayerful and tearful excursion for Helena.

It was time. The screeching sound was almost deafening as the old clanging passenger train came to an abrupt stop at Warsaw Central Train Station in Poland. Countless passengers had reached their destination. After regaining their balance, they got up from their seats, grabbed their belongings and travel bags, and quickly exited the train to head their separate ways.

However, it was an entirely different story for 19-year-old Helena. Without a stick of luggage and wearing the one and only dress she decided to bring on this spontaneous trip, she slowly made her way down the steep metal train steps. She felt utterly perplexed, when in a flash, stabbing fear overpowered her.

"What am I to do?" Helena quickly pondered.

Wide-eyed, she watched as other passengers emerged from the train and quickly scattered in all directions, like water spattered on a hot griddle. Unlike the others, Helena had no clue where she was going. In fact, she did not have a single plan! That is, except for following Jesus' instructions.

Where to turn

"To whom should I turn, as I know no one?"[16] Helena wracked her brain.

All alone, in a city of a million people, and not knowing even one single soul there, did this unseasoned traveler make a mistake? Well, Helena did know one thing for certain. She absolutely and unmistakably needed a beloved mother's help. Quickly, Helena turned her thoughts and heart to beseech the Blessed Mother.

"Mary, lead me, guide me." That was Helena's simple, yet sincere and earnest plea.

Immediately, Helena heard the Mother of God's words directing her. This very moment became an integral starting chapter of a remarkable holy journey. Helena had followed her heart and Jesus' guidance thus far, and now she needed to heed the further directions from Mary.

"I heard these words within me telling me to leave the town and to go to a certain nearby village where I would find a safe lodging for the night. I did so and found, in fact, that everything was just as the Mother of God told me."[17] Helen would later record these words in her *Diary*.

Helena got up early the following morning to head back to Warsaw where she entered the first church she could find. It turned out to be St. James Church at Grojecka Street in Ochota, a suburb of Warsaw. The pious young run-away got on her knees and prayed for God's will. She also noticed that Masses were being celebrated there one after the other.

She recalled, "During one of them I heard the words: **Go to that priest and tell him everything; he will tell you what to do next**." After the final blessing of Mass, Helena found her way to the sacristy. She did just as Jesus had told her to do. She told the priest what she was doing there, what had taken place in her soul, and asked his advice: "where to take the veil, in which religious order."[18]

God provides

At first, the priest was surprised at this stranger's request. And the saint-in-the-making expected that the priest she just met could simply tell her to which convent she should visit. It wasn't going to be that easy. Yet, Fr. James Dabrowski had recently been asked by his friends, Samuel and Aldona Lipszycowa, that if he came across a suitable candidate to work for them as a domestic, to send her over. They were of Jewish descent and were baptized in an earlier generation. Samuel was an agricultural engineer and central government official. The family lived on the edge of a forest preserve in Ostrowek, about 25 miles from Warsaw where Father had previously served as a parish priest.

This request being fresh on his mind, Fr. Dabrowski directed Helena to the family. First though, he gave her some very encouraging words. He told her that she should have strong confidence in God and He would provide for her future.

"For the time being, I shall send you to a pious lady with whom you will stay until you enter a convent,"[19] Fr. Dabrowski said. God must have surely inspired him, because his recommendation to live there turned out to be the perfect answer to Helena's perplexing question. Plus, as we will soon learn, Helena needed a place to stay and to work before she could actually cross over the threshold into religious life. It was to be a bit of a journey getting into the convent.

Even though entering religious life would take a bit more time, we can already see that God was providing for Helena, just as Father had said. Only the day prior, stepping off the train in Warsaw, she was all alone. Now, Helena knew someone — Fr. Dabrowski, and soon, a new family where she would have immediate lodging.

Soon enough, on July 1, 1924, Helena was standing outside the Lipszycowa family's front door, awaiting the door to be opened. Her freckled face was glowing and her auburn hair was tied up in a plait braid. She held onto all of her belongings, tied up in a small bundle in a headscarf.

Aldona Lipszycowa opened the door with a smile and received Helena with great kindness. It was an answer to Aldona's needs to have this strong, cheerful young woman's help at her home. Aldona would later say that she loved Helena's cheerfulness and joyful laughter, and the way in which she played with the children. Helena also knew well how to cook and clean. She learned much from her mother Marianna and her skills made her an excellent maid.

Aldona learned a Eucharistic hymn, "The Hidden Jesus" (*"Jesus Ukrytego"*), from Helena because she heard it sung by her so often as she cared for the children. We can imagine it played over and over in Aldona's head.

> I am to worship Jesus, hidden in the Blessed Sacrament.
> I am to give all to Him, His love my life to live.
> He wholly gives Himself to us, among us He did dwell.
> To His divine praise, let us devote our lives to Him.

It's interesting to note that Aldona later rescued Jews from death during the Second World War, risking her own life by doing so. She had grown fond of them when a student at a private Catholic school where she had several Jewish friends. Kind-hearted Aldona hid the Jews at her farm house in Ostrowek which was close to the railway line to the extermination camp in Treblinka. Escapees sometimes jumped off the train and made their way a mile through the woods to her house. She gave them lodging, food, and a railway ticket to safety.

Getting there

Back to Helena. Settling in at new employment could be somewhat stressful and surely Helena prayed that she would fit in and that everything would work out well in living and working at the Lipszycowa's. She was acutely aware her new position was a huge step towards her religious life.

Helena let Aldona know that she planned to work for her long enough to earn enough money for entrance into a convent. While living there, in her spare time, Helena visited convents to inquire about joining the congregation. She knew for sure that one of them had to the right one. After all, Jesus succinctly told her she would enter a convent. She trusted Him with all her heart.

Helena settled in well with the Lipszycowa family and stayed there for a while. We can assume it was a bit over a year, as we will soon understand. Helena wrote a letter to her parents and explained her plan to save money for the postulant's wardrobe and then enter a convent.

Helena enjoyed caring for the children and helping Aldona with whatever she needed. The family loved her and had confidence in her care of the children. Aldona didn't fully understand Helena's firm wholehearted commitment to join religious life. Because of her lack of understanding about the happiness to be found in religious life, there were times when Aldona tried to be a matchmaker for Helena, thinking that marriage and family life would suit her well. Though, Aldona was correct that Helena had every fine trait to become an excellent wife and mother, this is not what Helena was called by God to aspire to.

Sometime during Helena's employment at the Lipszycowa's home, Helena's sister Genevieve was sent by their parents to visit Helena. The two sisters were happy to see one another, but Genevieve's sole mission was to persuade her sister to come back home with her. Helena was not going to budge from her decision and holy commitment. Eventually, Genevieve relented her pressure when she realized there was no changing her determined sister's mind! Marianna and Stanislaus were very disappointed to see Genevieve arrive back home by herself.

God was lavish with His graces

We can imagine that at this point in Helena's life, Helena was acutely aware that big changes were on the horizon and that she needed to work and pray hard. She noted in her *Diary*, sometime later, that she experienced struggles.

She wrote, "At that time I had to struggle with many difficulties, but God was lavish with His graces. An ever greater longing for God began to take hold of me." Helena deeply yearned for God. She cried out to Him often in prayer. She felt His consolations in the way in which He bestowed His graces upon her. He was preparing her for a great work.

Helena wrote, "I sensed that I had a heart so big that nothing would be capable of filling it. And so I turned with all the longing of my soul to God."[20]

During the octave of Corpus Christi, on June 25, 1925, during a Vespers service, God touched Helena's soul in a very profound way. She described it like this: "God filled my soul with the interior light of a deeper knowledge of Him as Supreme Goodness and Supreme Beauty." She was enlightened about His tremendous love for her. She recalled, "I came to know how very much God loves me. Eternal is His love for me."

Just then, Helena made a spontaneous and special vow to God. She wrote: "It was at vespers — in simple words, which flowed from the heart, I made to God, a vow of perpetual chastity. From that moment I felt a greater intimacy with God, my Spouse. From that moment I set up a little cell in my heart where I always kept company with Jesus."[21]

God was powerfully moving in Helena's heart during her stay at the Lipszycowa's home. And Helena responded to God's grace with abundant love and even a special vow to Him.

Knocking on convent doors

Whenever Helena had time off from her domestic duties, she went into Warsaw to knock on convent doors. Each time she tried, she was rejected. We can imagine what these refusals did to her self-esteem. It wasn't her fault that she was from a poor peasant family and had very little formal education.

Truth be told, Helena was very smart, cheerful, and a hard worker. Still, the religious superiors frowned upon candidates from a "low rung" of society. They would be too much trouble at the convent, they surmised. On top of that, as we have learned already, she didn't have money for her postulant clothing and the convents were not wealthy. They expected the candidates to come to them with the required amount of money for clothing, and also, in most cases, a dowry of money too.

Despite all of the charms, gifts, and skills of Helena, it seemed that no convent wanted her. One Sister even said she was "Nothing extraordinary." That would be Mother Margaret Gimbutt's succinct summation of her impression of Helena. She didn't reveal her opinion to Helena. However, the young aspiring candidate felt crushed over the many doors closing in her face.

Later on, Helena recorded in her *Diary* about being accepted by Aldona and rejected by the convents. She wrote, "When I called on this lady, she received me very kindly. During the time I stayed with her, I was looking for a convent, but at whatever convent door I knocked, I was turned away. Sorrow gripped my heart, and I said to the Lord Jesus, 'Help me; don't leave me alone.'"[22]

We will soon learn how Helena coped with these rejections and how our Lord answered her earnest prayer. But first, let's think about a few things.

Something to Think About

Take a few minutes to think about Helena's incredible journey. She experienced great difficulties to pursue her desire and her calling to enter religious life. Even her pious parents were an obstacle. Yet, Helena was visited by Jesus Himself! So, she knew she needed to follow through with His requests of her. What would you do when faced with many rejections?

Think about how Helena turned to the Blessed Mother when she didn't know where to go. The Blessed Mother instructed her. Mary is our Mother, given to us by Jesus when He hung from the Cross at His crucifixion. Mary is a great gift to us and will always lead us to do the right thing — and always to her Son Jesus. We need to call upon her in our prayers.

Take a minute to think about your own life and how and when you can turn to Jesus and Mary. In addition, consider praying regularly to St. Faustina to ask for her intercession.

 Pray

Dear Jesus and Mary, please guide me. Help me to always seek Your holy will and not my own will. Jesus, I trust in You! Dear St. Faustina, please pray for me.

 A Merciful Action

Sometime soon, offer a few prayers for a complete stranger who might be lost or struggling in some way.

As elated as Helena was to finally be in the convent and immersed in a life of "Paradise" (as she had described it), she quickly became discouraged.

4

A Dream Come True

"At last I knocked on our door."[23] These words were written in black ink and neatly scrawled across a page of St. Faustina's *Diary*. We will discuss more about her *Diary* later on. For now, we will focus on what led up to her writing her recollections in the first place, and specifically, how Helena finally managed to get herself into a convent.

In our earlier chapter, Helena had expressed her deep sorrow because all of the convent doors were being shut on her. Every one she visited turned out to be a, "No." At those times, Helena might have sadly recalled her father's and mother's flat out, "No!" She was indeed feeling sorrowful because as much as she tried her best, it was not working.

Thus far, not one of the superiors in religious life wanted Helena, for she was not very significant, coming from a poor background and not having much education. The Mother superiors thought she would be more trouble to them than of help. She was a very unlikely religious candidate.

Still, Helena mustered up the courage and determination to go out and try again. No doubt, God granted the graces to her to persevere. He had His eye on her. But she in turn, needed to move her will (and her body!) and also she needed to trust that God would see her through. Off she went!

Helena's dream came true!

It was the summer of 1924, and Helena made her way to the door of the convent of the Congregation of the Sisters of Our Lady of Mercy. It was at 3/9 Zytnia Street in Warsaw. Though Helena did not know anything about these sisters, she knocked on the door and was welcomed inside by the portress Sr. Clara Himmer, who then went to the Mother General Leonardo Cielecka. Mother Margaret Gimbutt was also called for. After a short meeting with Helena, Mother Malgorzata returned to the Superior and reported that the person at the door was "no one special."

She also sort of complained that the visitor lacked a dowry and money for a trousseau (clothing for postulancy), she also said Helena was a bit too old, that she was only a domestic and cook by trade, and she was too frail. Basically, the Mother had nothing good to say about Helena. Thankfully, Helena did not overhear her negative report to the others. Otherwise, Helena might have become deeply saddened, since it did not look very promising.

Well, after all this, the votes were in and Helena did not make a very favorable impression with this Congregation. However, something quickly changed opinions. It began with Mother Michaela Moraczewska, the Mother Superior of the Zytnia convent (she became the Mother General of the entire Congregation shortly after in 1928). Mother Michaela entered into the conversation. She had been clandestinely watching Helena through a slightly opened parlor door and was not at all impressed at first.

Watching from the doorway Mother Moraczewska felt Helena exhibited a "somewhat unkempt external appearance."[24] She planned to send her away, albeit it in a charitable manner. Suddenly, she realized she should be more charitable and not seem rash in her decision. Before sending her away, she decided to take just a few minutes to ask Helena a few token questions.

Mother Moraczewska asked to see Helena in person. The two met in the parlor and Helena instantly liked Mother Moraczewska. She later described her as "permeated with divine light and very loving of God."[25]

It was within those few parlor minutes, which Mother thought was going to be a simple placation, that something unexpected and extraordinary happened. Mother Moraczewska began to like Helena! Her first impression had quickly changed. During those moments together, Mother became aware of some very fine attributes Helena possessed. After all, Helena's shining sincere smile, her simplicity, honesty, and apparent common sense burst through. And Mother Moraczewska decided to accept her.

Can we even imagine the great joy Helena soon felt in her heart when she learned her dream would come true in her acceptance into religious life? Even though this was an absolute major breakthrough, it was not a simple task to walk through the door of religious life and begin. Certain requirements needed to be put into place.

First of all, Jesus would have to agree! Yes, you read that correctly. I really said, "Jesus!" We will soon see. After Jesus' agreement, Helena could only enter religious life after she worked in the world and raised enough money for her trousseau which would pay for her postulant clothing. The Holy See eventually waived the dowry that was usually required to enter religious life.

Here's what transpired: After Mother Michaela met with Helena, she instructed her to see "the Lord of the house" and ask Him if He accepted her into their Congregation. It's possible that sending the young lady to the chapel gave Mother Michaela a little bit more time to put her thoughts together and think of exactly what she would say to Helena about the acceptance and the requirements.

The hopeful aspirant happily agreed to go to the chapel and off she went! Later on, Helena told the story this way: "When the Mother Superior, the present Mother General Michael came out to meet me, she told me, after a short conversation, to go to the Lord of the house and ask whether He would accept me." Helena knew right away what Mother Michaela meant. "The Lord of the house" was Jesus in the Blessed Sacrament.

"I understood at once that I was to ask this of the Lord Jesus. With great joy, I went to the chapel and asked Jesus: 'Lord of this house, do You accept me? This is how one of these sisters told me to put the question to You.'"

We can sense the honest and sincere simplicity in which Helena approaches Jesus. She trusts that He is there in the Blessed Sacrament — and that He is listening. And also that He will give an answer to her.

Helena recorded in her Diary, "Immediately I heard this voice: **I do accept; you are in My Heart**." Helena reported back to the Mother Superior. "When I returned from the chapel, Mother Superior asked first of all, 'Well, has the Lord accepted you?'" Helena responded, "Yes." Mother Michaela replied, "If the Lord has accepted, then I also will accept."[26]

Working hard for religious life

What a dream come true for Helena to hear Mother Michael speak those words to her! Helena had already worked exceptionally hard to get this far. After all, she had struggled deeply due to her parent's flat out refusal for her to enter religious life — she was not simply disappointed, she was worried about their feelings of rejection and heartache they must have experienced when she did, in fact, launch out into the unknown in search of a convent. It was immensely difficult for her to be disobedient to their wishes, especially since she had always been obedient to them.

In addition, Helena had knocked on many doors and sorrowfully suffered due to the continual refusals. Then, she tried once again to make a good impression with the Mother Superior of what would turn out to be the final convent. That certainly wasn't easy, but our Lord must have provided many graces so that minds and opinions would change so dramatically. Mother Michael had initially said, "No, she is not for us!"[27]

However, even with Mother Michael's acceptance, as was mentioned, Helena needed to continue working hard to achieve her goal and calling. Mother Michael bid good bye to Helena after instructing her to bring the earned money to the convent for safe keeping which she would save for her trousseau. Helena decided to stay on with Aldona and her family. It was the perfect solution. Helena was already established with the family, who was very fond of her and treated her like a member of their family. Helena continued to earn money to save up for her trousseau. Since Helena was very conscientious, deeply desiring to enter religious life, she spent very little of her earnings on herself so she could save as much money as possible.

Some months later, she stopped at the Warsaw convent of the Congregation of the Sisters of Our Lady of Mercy to give to them a sum of money to hold onto for safekeeping her trousseau. She kept her promise to Mother Michael. However, when Mother was reached by letter when she was in Vilnius, she had already forgotten about the freckle-faced young lady with the winning smile who almost didn't get accepted by her. However, her mind was refreshed and she must have been pleased that Helena had kept her promise. The young aspirant continued to carry on adding to the trousseau savings.

The difficult time finally arrived to part ways. Helena had saved several hundred *zloty* which was enough for her postulant wardrobe. This milestone of finally making the leap from employment to entering the convent was supposed to be brimming with the greatest joy for Helena. However, the experience of separating from Aldona and her family was extremely tough for Aldona, her family and for Helena. They had grown very close and had become a kind of family. God surely placed them together for an important time in Helena's life.

Though Aldona was well aware that Helena would be with her family for only a period of time, still, it was actually a "harrowing experience" for Aldona, as she later recalled. She said Helena had become "so intimate" with her family and they had become so attached to her. Surely, it was the same for kind-hearted Helena. She was dearly thankful for the many blessings of being intimately entwined with the family for more than a year. So much happened in that time together while Helena watched the kids grow and mature, as well as welcome a new Lipszycowa baby into the world.

But it was time to leave. Helena sincerely promised the family she would never forget them.

All about mercy

To give a little bit of historical background of the Congregation Helena entered, I'll mention that there were many congregations of women religious that came into existence in Poland in the mid nineteenth century. It's interesting to learn how the Congregation that Helena joined actually came into being. The religious community of Mother Thérèse Rondeau in Laval, France was the inspiration for the Sisters of Our Lady of Mercy.

Both these congregations were instituted for personal sanctification for the nuns, but also to assist women who were living on the margins of society — women who made grave mistakes but wanted to change their lives. Later on, wayward girls were also accepted. The sisters were to imitate Christ in His mercy and help to rehabilitate souls. They were specifically devoted to the Patroness of the entire Congregation, Mary, Mother of Mercy and to the Mercy of God, which is the inspiration of the Congregation's apostolic work. However, the religious congregation part was not exactly in the original plan!

Here's what happened: It turns out that a certain Countess Vladislav Potocka, who became a childless widow after 17 years of marriage, decided to spend the rest of her life serving God and doing works of mercy. She had a deep desire to help women, who she felt were lost and needed help to get their lives in order. Her spiritual director Fr. Zygmunt Golan suggested that she visit with and learn from the religious community of Mother Thérèse Rondeau in Laval, France which helped wayward women and girls, who they described as "morally fallen."

The Countess closely observed the sisters' techniques and procedures and was very impressed and learned quite a bit, at the same time, felt inspired to do more. She returned to Poland. With permission, she ended up kind of borrowing the Constitution and apostolic charism from the French religious community and used it to form a new congregation. Because of this "borrowing," of charism and Constitution, Mother Thérèse Rondeau is considered a co-foundress of the new Congregation which is the Sisters of Our Lady of Mercy. The Countess called herself Mother Teresa Potocka.

As it happened, each of these congregations' founders often referred to a French aristocrat Thérèse de Lamourous, who had established a "House of Mercy" in 1801, after the French Revolution. Both of the foundresses (Poland and France) initially simply aimed to help the women in need and were not at all thinking of starting a religious congregation. However, God had other plans! Everything unfolded as it should.

Archbishop Felenski invited Mother Teresa Potocka to take over a run-down building and turn it into a shelter. This is the place where the Sisters of Our Lady of Mercy began.

The Congregation of the Sisters of Our Lady of Mercy, of which Helena was accepted was officially founded on November 1, 1862 when Mother Potocka and her companions opened the first House of Mercy at Zytnia Street in Warsaw. Saint Zygmunt Szczesny Felinski, the archbishop of Warsaw at that time (now a saint) consecrated the center.

Over the moon!

Back to Helena. Hallelujah! The door behind Helena now slammed shut! She was now inside! Helena entered the Warsaw convent on August 1, 1925 and began her postulancy, which is a trial period in religious life. It was the eve of the Feast of Our Lady of the Angels that she finally and exuberantly crossed over the threshold into religious life! "At last the time came when the door of the convent was opened for me," she later expressed. She was over the moon with excitement and thanksgiving to God.

Helena expressed, "I felt immensely happy; it seemed to me that I had stepped into the life of Paradise." The deepest desire of her heart ever since she was a child had finally become a reality. Now, she had to pass a few exams and see how it worked out. The superiors would be keeping a very close eye on Helena.

She also expressed, "A single prayer bursting forth from my heart, one of thanksgiving."[28] Helena was a very appreciative young lady.

Aspirant to Postulant

Two older sisters examined Helena and passed her first examination. This confirmed that she was free from obstacles getting in the way of entering religious life. In addition, they determined that she possessed the necessary attributes of body and soul to live a religious life. After passing that stage, Helena was officially an aspirant and became a postulant. This meant that she was to go through a trial period in religious life. The sisters would be watching her and Helena would see how she liked this lifestyle and discern if she wanted to remain in the Congregation. The postulancy would be the first of several stages before becoming an official Sister in the Congregation. It could last between three and six months.

She received dark clothing, but not yet a religious habit, and she wore a short veil. Helena slept in a dormitory with other sisters whose cells were divided by white curtains. The Congregation of nuns was divided into two choirs, or two parts. The first choir was for the educated sisters who did educational work with the girls. The second choir consisted of the uneducated young women from lower levels of society. They did all of the support work, such as cooking, cleaning, gardening, and answering the door or gate. Every sister, no matter which choir, was responsible for the salvation of all souls entrusted to their care through prayer, and possibly also with good works.

To which choir do you think Helena was placed? The second choir! That is because she was basically uneducated and was a peasant. Her first job was in the kitchen. She worked under Sr. Sabina Tronina. Helena worked very hard in the kitchen. She didn't mind doing the work, but she began to wonder why there was not enough time scheduled for prayer. She often inquired of Sr. Sabrina if she could go to the chapel.

Helena was also assigned to clean the room of Mother Jane Barkiewicz (a former superior and Vicar General of the Congregation), as well as take care of her whenever she was ill. Mother Jane was also keeping her eye on the new postulant. Upon observing Helena, Mother Jane one time had said, "Helen is an interior soul."[29] Mother Jane was also the directress of the postulants and had a reputation for being demanding and often created an atmosphere of fear.

Trouble in Paradise

As elated as Helena was to finally be in the convent and immersed in a life of "Paradise" (as she had described it), she quickly became discouraged. Only three weeks in the convent and she began to think she should leave and seek out a stricter convent that would be more rigorously focused on prayer. She felt that with all of her other responsibilities, there was too little time devoted to prayer. Helena also felt there were "many other things which spoke to my soul in favor of entering a religious community of a stricter observance." She said these things "took a firm hold" of her soul.

Could the evil one have been tempting Helena to give up what she had long worked for? Helena said this temptation or thought, "was growing stronger and stronger to the point where I decided one day to announce my departure." Helena planned to "definitely leave" the convent. Helena would meet with the Mother Superior the next day. Or, so she thought! Before retiring for the night, she went off to the chapel to spend a little time with Jesus. She desired from Him a better understanding of this troubling experience which continued to gnaw at her heart.

Helena asked Jesus when in the chapel, but ended up even more confused. This is how Helena described what happened after she asked Him for light in this matter: "But I received nothing in my soul except a strange unrest which I did not understand." Even so, she made a decision. She recalled, "I made up my mind to approach Mother Superior the next morning right after Mass and tell her of my decision."[30]

It turned out that Jesus had another plan. After leaving the chapel, Helena went to her cell. She felt full of anguish and discontent. She later wrote, "I did not know what to do with myself. I threw myself headlong on the ground and began to pay fervently that I might come to know the will of God." She continued, "There is silence everywhere as in the tabernacle. All the sisters are resting like white hosts enclosed in Jesus' chalice. It is only from my cell that God can hear the moaning of a soul. I did not know that one was not allowed to pray in the cell after nine without permission."

Sorrowful Jesus appears

Suddenly, a startling brightness filled Helena's cell. On the white curtain divider of her cell appeared the very sorrowful Face of Jesus! Helena was astounded and alarmed to see this. She felt very sad for Jesus. She recalled vividly, "large tears were falling on my bedspread. Not knowing what all this meant, I asked Jesus, 'Jesus, who has hurt You so?'"

Jesus immediately answered Helena. **"It is you who will cause Me this pain if you leave this convent. It is to this place that I called you and nowhere else; and I have prepared many graces for you."** Can we even imagine how Helena felt hearing this from her Lord and Savior?

Helena's mind and heart immediately changed. She would not leave and she fervently begged pardon from Jesus for not fully trusting Him. She was able to bring all of this experience to the Confessional the following day, telling the priest everything that had taken place in her soul. The priest assured her that God made Himself very clear and that Helena was to remain in the Congregation. He told her that she should never again think of leaving for another religious order. God unquestionably wanted her there. Helena stated, "From that moment on, I have always felt happy and content."[31] There was no more indecision about where Helena was supposed to be.

After this ordeal, and having gone through all of the partings and changes required of her to enter religious life, as well as her intense spiritual zeal and also conflicts, Helena's health began to decline and she fell ill from exhaustion. She was sent away for a time. We will soon learn where she went and about the amazing things that happened during her convalescence. But first, let's ponder a few things.

Something to Think About

Take a few minutes to reflect upon what you have learned in this chapter. Think about Helena's perseverance in the midst of contradiction and disappointment. What did she do when she was in doubt or feeling discouraged? She kept going, with God's grace. She knew it was important to turn to God in prayer. She humbled herself to ask for help and knew that she did not know all of the answers, but God would. She also trusted as much as she could that God would eventually reveal His holy will to her.

It is the same with you and me. We should always turn to God in prayer, especially when we are troubled, sad, or confused. We can also turn to a trusted relative or friend.

Take a moment to ponder the hard work of Helena. She was determined to enter religious life and worked hard to earn the necessary money. Helena was also very appreciative to finally achieve her life-long goal and dream to enter the convent. She got on her knees and thanked God. Think about your own life. Do you thank God enough? Are you appreciative for His many blessings?

Pray

Dear Jesus and Mary, please guide me. Jesus, I trust in You! Thank You for all of Your many blessings! Dear St. Faustina, please pray for me.

A Merciful Action

Do your best to offer kind words to someone for whom you don't particularly care. If possible, do an anonymous kind deed for someone.

She couldn't take her eyes off of Him and saw clearly that, "From beneath the garment, slightly drawn aside at the breast, there were emanating two large rays, one red, the other pale." (*Diary*, 47).

5

A Grand Mission Revealed to a "Nobody"

Helena recalled in her *Diary*, "The dear Mother Superior sent me with two other sisters for a rest in Skolimow, not far from Warsaw."[32] At the Congregation's rented summer country home, Helena got a change of scenery and a chance to recuperate from the physical and spiritual exhaustion she experienced. This home was used by the Congregation for the sisters living in Warsaw and the girls in their charge.

While resting there, Helena was only involved in light duties. She cooked for the other sisters and herself and also took care of one convalescing nun. Very soon after arriving at the home, Helena took another trip.

A trip to Purgatory

Helena felt inspired to ask Jesus for whom she should pray. Jesus told her He would reveal that to her on the following night. The young postulant experienced something amazingly incredible which included her guardian angel and learning about the special souls who needed prayers — and, as I mentioned, another trip!

However, this was no ordinary excursion. The young nun recalled it this way: "I saw my Guardian Angel, who ordered me to follow him. In a moment I was in a misty place full of fire in which there was a great crowd of suffering souls." Can we even imagine this? Helena was escorted to Purgatory so she would understand for whom Jesus wanted her to pray.

She continued, "They were praying fervently, but to no avail, for themselves; only we can come to their aid." Helena learned that the Holy Souls in Purgatory pray for us, but once they are in Purgatory, they can no longer pray for themselves.

She wrote, "The flames which were burning them did not touch me at all. My Guardian Angel did not leave me for an instant." As extraordinarily unbelievable (albeit a bit scary) this journey was for Helena, she had no reason to fear because her guardian angel kept her safe.

Helena asked the souls an important question. She wanted to know what their greatest suffering was. She noted it in her *Diary*. "They answered me in one voice that their greatest torment was longing for God."

We know through official Church teaching that the Holy Souls in Purgatory will definitely reach Heaven one day, but they must be purified in Purgatory first. We can read this in the *Catechism of the Catholic Church* (1030 to 1032). Even though the Holy Souls realize they will one day finally see the Face of God, they still suffer immensely with their feeling of longing for God.

Helena saw Mother Mary visiting the Holy Souls in Purgatory. She later wrote in her *Diary*, "I saw Our Lady visiting the souls in Purgatory. The souls call her 'The Star of the Sea.' She brings them refreshment." Helena was very intrigued by details of Purgatory. However, as much as much as Helena wanted to visit a bit longer and talk with the Holy Souls more, it was time to leave.

She recalled, "I wanted to talk with them some more, but my Guardian Angel beckoned me to leave. We went out of that prison of suffering." As Helena left that supernatural and sobering place, she heard an interior voice:

"My Mercy does not want this, but justice demands it."

That extraordinary visit to Purgatory enlightened Helena about the truths of that holy place of purification and also the important need to pray for the Holy Souls. She later wrote in her *Diary*, "Since that time, I am in closer communion with the suffering souls."[33]

Though Helena felt in closer communion to these special souls after that experience, at the time of that amazing visit, she had absolutely no idea about what would happen in the future when the Holy Souls in Purgatory needed her prayers. We will discuss that later on. For now, let's delve into early convent life.

Humiliations, contradictions, and suffering

When we think about religious life, we might consider it as totally blessed and overflowing with only good things: a rich and holy lifestyle, as well as necessary helpful rules and regulations. After all, it is a life of prayer, service, and virtue while striving to get to Heaven one day. We might also believe that religious life should be blissful because we are dealing with, in a sense, heavenly things.

However, like all endeavors, vocations, and occupations, work and effort must be put forth in order to achieve a goal. Many times, the work is arduous. In addition, there may be obstacles or contradictions involved, especially in religious life. That is because the spiritual battle is extra fierce in this realm. The evil one always seeks to make us fail and to discourage us in the process. But we should never fear his tricks. Instead, we can pray for God's guidance and many graces to be attentive to the battle and to overcome the difficulties. However, we can never do it alone. We must always seek God's help.

Religious life was not just handed to Helena on a silver platter. As we know, she had to fight for it. At first, she thought she had entered "Paradise" when finally stepping freely into the convent. But truth be told, convent life for Helena was not a bowl of cherries. In addition to hard work and perseverance to get into the convent, other difficulties were in store for Helena — ones she never imagined. There would be humiliations, contradictions, criticisms, and more suffering on the horizon.

Some of the sisters mocked Helena because of her purity and great love for Jesus. We would think that other like-minded people would be supportive of one another. However, a fallen human nature and faults can cause problems within relationships. Helena later wrote about some of the humiliations in her *Diary*. One time, a Mother Superior told her that the Lord wouldn't want to associate with her.

Specifically, Helena wrote:

> One of the Mothers [probably Mother Jane], when
> she learned about my close relationship with the Lord

Jesus, told me that I must be deluding myself. She told me that the Lord Jesus associates in this way only with saints and not with sinful souls "like you Sister!" After that it was as if I mistrusted Jesus. In one of my morning talks with Him I said, "Jesus, are You not an illusion?" Jesus answered me, **My love deceives no one.**[34]

Just before she finally professed her vows — something Helena had lovingly long awaited — a certain sister told Helena flat out that she would prevent her from doing so.

"Sister, you will not be going for the third probation. I myself will see to it that you will not be permitted to make your vows."[35] What did Helena do? She kept quiet and concealed her pain even though the Sister's words cut right through her.

Well, the threatening Sister was not able to stand in the way of God's plan. Later on, Sr. Faustina reflected on the contradictions and hurtful experiences. She came to realize that God has His reasons for everything.

She neatly scrawled in her *Diary*:

In prayer I always find light and strength of spirit although there are moments so trying and hurtful, that it is sometimes difficult to imagine that these things can happen in a convent. Strangely, God sometimes allows them, but always in order to manifest or develop virtue in a soul. That is the reason for trials.[36]

Helena endured much. Thankfully, she saw glimpses of hope and light here and there. And Jesus Himself spoke to her heart. As we know, Helena had already been tempted to leave the convent after only a few weeks there. The spiritual conflicts she endured impacted her physical health. That is why the Mother Superior sent her away for a while to the Congregation's summer home in Skolimów.

After a time of rest in Skolimów, Helena was transferred back to Warsaw where she was assigned to work in the kitchen.

Kitchen table humility

One evening after dinner, Helena thought she'd surely die of shame. A certain Sr. Marcianna Oswiecimska, who was the cook at the time, became very irritated with Helena. She asked Helena to wash the dishes after dinner. Helena was happy to oblige. She never minded helping. In fact, she was eager to help and knew that when she was obedient, she was pleasing Jesus. She always tried to do all of her work as well as she possibly could in order to be extra pleasing to God.

As she washed the dishes, some sisters came in late for dinner and Helena set down her dish cloth to serve dinner to them. She then went back to the dirty dishes in the sink. We can imagine Helena's surprise when Sr. Marcianna walked in and suddenly gave her a strange penance for not washing the dishes as quickly as she had expected her to do. Perhaps "shock" is a better word.

Here's what happened: Sister Marcianna returned to the kitchen and observed that the dishes were not all washed. She ordered Helena to sit on a kitchen table. That's correct — it was *on* a table. The Sister cook told her it was a penance for not finishing the job.

Well, that was a hard enough punishment to just sit there, not able to help, while Sr. Marainna was at the sink scrubbing away. But on top of that embarrassing punishment, Helena was not allowed to talk or defend herself. She was ordered to just sit there quietly! This was so difficult because other sisters came into the kitchen when Helena was sitting atop the table! Add to that, they saw Sr. Marianna doing the dishes!

Doesn't seem fair, does it? It was excruciating for the young postulant to bear the embarrassment. She was unfairly punished and also criticized. In that moment, she might have reminisced about her family life back home and how her parents had never treated her or her siblings unfairly. Yet, ironically in religious life, a time meant to grow close to God, unthinkable things occurred.

About eight years later, Helena recalled the daunting experience of Sr. Marcianna getting upset with her and ordering her to sit on the table while she did the dishes herself.

Helena wrote:

And while I was sitting there, the sisters came along and were astounded to find me sitting on the table, and each one had her say. One said that I was a loafer and another, "What an eccentric!" I was a postulant at the time. Others said, "What kind of sister will she make?" Still, I could not get down because sister had ordered me to sit there by virtue of obedience until she told me to get down. Truly, God alone knows how many acts of self-denial it took. I thought I'd die of shame. [37]

Helena later pondered, "God often allowed such things for the sake of my inner formation, but He compensated me for this humiliation by a great consolation." It was at Benediction when she was blessed with Jesus' profound words. Helena recalled that she saw "Him in great beauty." She wrote, "Jesus looked at me kindly and said, **My daughter, do not be afraid of sufferings; I am with you.**"[38]

We can only imagine the profound peace that entered her soul because of Jesus' words. In time, Helena came to know that Jesus allowed her to experience certain sufferings and humiliations in order for her to grow in holiness as He lovingly burnished her heart and soul as a metalsmith did to shape, forge, and perfect a precious metal.

Jesus desired that Helena turn to Him during such times. As difficult as it was for Helena to receive Sr. Marianna's punishment that day, the young postulant certainly turned to Jesus and made what she called "many acts of self-denial." She continued to offer the humiliation up to Jesus, asking for His help. Helena grew to accept her sufferings as gifts from God. Jesus later taught her that meditating upon His suffering during His Passion would advance her in holiness. It's the same for all of us.

An oasis in the desert

Helena was so happy to see Aldona, her former employer and mother figure a couple of times after Helena went away to religious life. Once was in the fall of 1925, when Aldona visited the young religious when she was at the convent on Zytnia Street. At that time, Helena had a few moments to share with Aldona that she was deeply struggling. Aldona wanted to scoop her up and bring her back to her home. It was hard for Aldona to see Helena unhappy. Even if it was that she was happy to be in the convent, Aldona could see there was a kind of discontentment in Helena. It puzzled her. She deeply desired that Helena be happy.

Later, before the end of Helena's postulancy, Aldona saw Helena again and observed her struggles, saddened to see the once jubilant carefree young lady under duress. That was on January 23, 1926, and Helena told Aldona she felt burdened but also felt sustained by divine grace. Again, Aldona wanted to bring Helena back home with her. According to Aldona, Helena told her that she was going to Kraków for her novitiate and would do her best, but if she couldn't persevere, she would return to Aldona and her children. We don't know for sure if Helena really meant this, or if she was simply trying to make Aldona feel better. She also told Aldona that she would persevere because Jesus wanted her to do so. She said she would obediently bear all the suffering because it was her greatest desire to please God.

Novitiate

After several months staying and studying in Warsaw, on January 23, 1926, Helena traveled to Lagiewniki, Kraków, to finish up her last three months of postulancy period of religious life. Helena and the other postulants would prepare for the novitiate, when they would receive their veil and habit, as well as their new name.

Something quite extraordinary happened the very day Helena arrived at the Kraków convent. It concerned a young nun in the second choir. We will discuss it in a little while.

April 30, 1926, was a very big day for Helena! It was the day of the solemn ceremony of receiving the religious habit and veil for the Congregation of the Sisters of Mercy in Kraków-Lagiewniki. Helena had worked very hard to enter the novitiate of religious life and this ceremony was to be a pivotal moment in her life. Helena expressed the incredible feelings she experienced upon entering this phase of religious life later on when she wrote in her *Diary*, "An inconceivable joy reigned in my soul."[39]

In addition to the veil, habit, and new name she received, Helena professed her first vows. Before she ultimately professed her final vows in religious life, she would profess vows twice more.

Mother Malgorzata was the directress of novices and presented the veil to Helena. Interestingly, just a couple of years prior to this day, Mother Malgorzata had negatively assessed Helena when she first approached the door of the convent to seek entrance. Mother had said the winsome young lady was "no one special."

Receiving the veil, habit and new name

When it was time for Helena to take her veil, Mother Malgorzata still did not realize just how special Helena actually was, and of course, had no way of knowing she would become an extraordinary saint in their Congregation. Most likely, she had observed Helena's pleasant disposition, her progress in the spiritual life, and her kindness to others in the Congregation. Nonetheless, she did not know of the depth of Helena's spiritual life and her love for Jesus, Mary, and the saints.

On that momentous day, Sr. Clemens Buczek was assigned to help Helena get ready at the altar. She helped Helena take off the gown that she had worn throughout postulancy so that she could don her new habit and veil for the first time. When the moment arrived for Helena to receive her veil and habit, Sr. Clemens started to rush her.

"Hurry up and put on the habit."[40]

Just as soon as Sr. Clemens uttered those words, Helena collapsed! Sister Clemens ran to get smelling salts to revive her. Sister Clemens must have thought that Helena fainted because she was nervous. Helena never let on what actually happened in that moment. That is, Jesus had revealed to Helena the arduous life of adversity in store for her. He did not yet reveal the great mission, but a profound foretaste of the suffering to come — all in one minute's time.

For years to come, Sr. Clemens teased Helena about the fainting incident. Poor Helena! However, she put up with the light ridicule with a smile and never revealed to Sister what actually occurred in her heart and soul. It wasn't until after Helena's death that Sr. Clemens found out the truth.

Helena recorded in her *Diary*, "The day I took the [religious] habit, God let me understand how much I was to suffer. I clearly saw to what I was committing myself. I experienced a moment of that suffering."[41] That is precisely why Helena fainted. She experienced a foretaste of the incredible suffering she would later endure in order to carry out the mammoth mission that was eventually entrusted to her.

God allows us to suffer at times for our own good and the good of others. In the cases of the great saints who were called to great missions, their suffering was quite intense. Sometimes, the pain dwelled in the fact that they were mocked, persecuted, or ridiculed, and disbelieved — even by the people who loved them. In other cases, the difficulties and suffering came from enemies of the Church. Jesus told us in the Bible, "If any want to become my followers, let them deny themselves and take up their cross and follow me" (Mt. 16:24).

It might sound impossible to do this, but God is a loving God. He grants many graces to us. After He revealed the future suffering to the saint-in-the-making at her solemn ceremony, He comforted her. She later wrote in her *Diary*, "But then God filled my soul again with great consolations."[42]

Sister Faustina is "born"

During the ceremony, Helena received her new name. She would no longer be called her baptismal name, "Helena." Father Stanislaus Rospond solemnly told her, "From today on, you will not be called by your baptismal name. You will be called Sr. Maria

Faustina."[43] Her name had been chosen by the Congregation's Superior General, Mother Leonarda Cielecka. Each new Sister receives two names. Maria, always the first name in honor of the Blessed Mother, the order's patroness.

On June 20, 1926, Sr. Faustina's first directress of novices, Mother Malgorzata Gimbutt was replaced by Mother Jozefa Brzoza. Mother Jozefa, an experienced nun, was an immense help to Sr. Faustina's spiritual life. She imparted to the young novice many simple, yet essential tips in the life of holiness, such as: to be simple, trusting, non-complaining, to be calm when others panic, to be thankful and to be pleased with everything. Mother Jozefa taught Sr. Faustina to strive to see everything in her life as a blessing from God and to pray for a childlike confidence in God. Mother Jozefa made a great impression on Sister Faustina and the young novice wrote about Mother's good counsel in her *Diary*.

From April 30, 1926 to April 30, 1928, Sr. Faustina stayed at the convent in Lagiewniki, Kraków, for the entire novitiate. She devoted time to prayer and also the work assigned to her. For the most part, Sr. Faustina worked in the convent's busy kitchen, often cooking and cleaning up for one hundred fifty people or more.

The Congregation took care of many girls and women (wards), from difficult backgrounds, educating, teaching the Catechism, and instilling prayer and good behavior in them. The Sisters also taught housework and farm work, as well as needlework, tailoring, and art to them. The wards also helped out in the bakeries, the gardens, and the convent laundries.

Darkness descended upon Faustina

As much as Sr. Faustina strove to be obedient, joyful, helpful, and exceedingly prayerful, she struggled through a strange aridity in prayer during a painful period of darkness in the spiritual life. This occurred at the end of her first year of the novitiate. No one knew of her interior sufferings because Faustina did not reveal them on the outside. She only disclosed it all to her mistress of novices and her director. During her dark nights, Sr.

Faustina no longer felt consoled in prayer. She meditated on holy things with great difficulty. Fear wrapped chains around her heart and the young nun doubted and became very confused. She felt miserable, to say the least. Even simple truths of the Faith confounded her.

It seemed as if all hell had broken loose. At one point Sr. Faustina felt absolutely sure that God had abandoned her. She questioned her faith. She wondered: Was it worth it to strive for virtue when she felt so awful? Doubt turned into feelings of despair. Poor Sr. Faustina even suffered the same hellish torments that damned souls experience.

Why did God allow this? Many saints have experienced a period of darkness along their path to sanctity. Saint John of the Cross coined a term "dark night of the senses" to describe the phenomenon suffered by the greatest of Christian mystics. Sister Faustina did not have an opportunity to read any of St. John of the Cross's writings. This sudden darkness was a perplexing mystery to her.

Thankfully, Mother Jozefa recognized this spiritual state of darkness and did her best to assure Sr. Faustina that God was in control and had destined her for great things and because He did, He entrusted her with this huge trial at such a young age.

Mother Jozefa consoled Sr. Faustina, "Know, dear Sister, that God has chosen you for great sanctity. This is a sign that God wants to have you very close to Himself in Heaven. Have great trust in the Lord Jesus."[44]

We can only imagine what young Faustina went through and how difficult it was for her to accept that the painful suffering she endured was actually from God, the very One she strove to draw near to. However, though her prayers felt as dry as the sands of the Sahara Desert, she continued to cry out to Jesus. He would get her through this. The young nun also realized and later wrote in her *Diary*, "God alone can test a soul in this way, because He alone knows what the soul can endure."[45]

Sister Faustina was being tested and purified, much as a gorgeous sparkling diamond needs to undergo extremely high temperatures and intense pressure for a period of time before it can become brilliant and beautiful. God continually supplied the graces for Sr. Faustina, even though she couldn't feel them.

Sister Faustina later recalled in her *Diary*:

> [F]ear began to sweep over me. Going deeper into myself, I could find nothing but great misery. I could also clearly see the great holiness of God. I did not dare to raise my eyes to Him, but reduced myself to dust under His feet and begged for mercy. My soul was in this state for almost six months. Our beloved Mother Directress encouraged me in these difficult moments. But this suffering continued to grow stronger.[46]

First vows

On October 30, 1928, Sr. Faustina made her first temporary profession of vows. She must have been very delighted that her dear parents came for this pivotal ceremony. They had not seen one another in four years. As much as Marianna and Stanislaus had protested their daughter going into the convent, they were now present to support her. Since all the rooms were taken up, Faustina's pious parents spent the night in the garden shed amid shovels and rakes. They did not sleep one wink — not because they were uncomfortable, but because they were up all night praying for their dear Helena.

At the time of her first vows, Faustina felt an ardent desire to totally empty herself "for God by an active love, but a love that would be imperceptible, even to the sisters closest to me."[47]

That day, Sr. Faustina took a little walk through the garden with her father. Stanislaus wondered if she was bored. He didn't understand that there existed a great beauty wrapped up in the monotony and structure of obedience in religious life. When he asked his daughter about her religious life she told him, "You see, Daddy, the One to Whom I made my vows is my Husband and your Son-in-law."[48] Deeply moved by his daughter's words, Stanislaus was finally at peace. He and his wife went back home to the family and continued to pray for their dear Helena.

Yet, even though Faustina gave herself completely to God during her vows, she still struggled with darkness. She later penned in her *Diary*:

> However, even after the vows, darkness continued to reign in my soul for almost half a year. Once, when I was praying, Jesus pervaded all my soul, darkness melted away, and I heard these words within me: **You are My joy; you are My heart's delight**. From that moment I felt the Most Holy Trinity in my heart; that is to say, within myself. I felt that I was inundated with Divine light. Since then, my soul has been in intimate communion with God, like a child with its beloved Father.[49]

The day after her vows, on October 31, 1928, Sr. Faustina returned to Zytnia Street. While there, Sister Faustina was in close contact with many of the wards since she was in the second choir of the Congregation and often assisted or taught the girls in the kitchen, or sometimes out in the garden. This convent housed 200 wards. The second choir sisters were very busy with their work there.

Sister Faustina took every opportunity to speak to the wards about God. She impressed upon them the importance of doing good and making small sacrifices for God. The young girls became fond of the young lovable nun with the bright demeanor. They respected her and enjoyed her company. Conversing with the engaging Sr. Faustina made their tasks seem a bit easier.

Thankfully, Faustina had some help from a certain sister named Sr. Krescencja Bogdanik who was appointed to be an aid, or what the sisters called an, "angel." Older sisters supported younger novices as they became accustomed to religious life. Sister Krescencja was very pleased with Sr. Faustina's outlook and childlike joy.

After making first vows, Sr. Faustina officially entered the Juniorate stage of her religious life. She moved around quite a bit during this period of five years, renewing each year until perpetual vows. During these years, Faustina stayed in many places:

on Zytnia Street, in Warsaw, in Vilnius, on Hetmanska Street, in Plock, in Biala, and in Walendow. Sister Faustina was so cooperative. Whenever a need arose, she was happy to accommodate and move into another convent to serve in whatever capacity was needed.

Saints attract saints

Sister Faustina's darkness grew worse. Sometime during Sr. Faustina's dark night, she decided to invoke the help of the saints by making novenas (usually nine days of prayer for specific intentions). The young nun already knew how efficacious novenas of prayer were and so she decided to make several novenas to various saints. She was especially attracted to St. Thérèse of the Child Jesus (1873-1897) and suddenly became inspired to make a novena to the French Carmelite. Faustina prayed to her with great fervor. Something incredibly unexpected occurred on the fifth day of the novena. That is, Sister Faustina had a conversation with her favorite saint!

It happened during a very vivid dream. Incidentally, St. Thérèse had also experienced a dark night in the spiritual life and she brought great consolation to Sr. Faustina, who asked the Little Flower (as St. Thérèse is often called) some direct questions about her spiritual life and about Eternal Life.

Here's how it happened according to Faustina's *Diary* entry: "On the fifth day of the novena, I dreamed of Saint Therese, but it was as if she were still living on earth." Saint Thérèse did not let on to Faustina that she was a saint. The Little Flower comforted Faustina and told her not to worry about the matter that afflicted her, but to trust God more. Then St. Thérèse revealed that she had "suffered greatly too." Sister Faustina doubted her.

Our friend Faustina said, "It seems to me that you have not suffered at all." Saint Thérèse explained that she indeed suffered much. She then stated to the young nun, "Sister, know that in three days the difficulty will come to a happy conclusion." Faustina still doubted. So, Thérèse revealed to her that she was a saint! Suddenly, Sr. Faustina's soul flooded with joy. She replied to St. Thérèse, "You are a saint?" Saint Thérèse assured her that she was. The Little Flower again explained, "Trust that this matter will be resolved in three days."

Sister Faustina was eager to know more. "Dear sweet Thérèse, tell me, shall I go to heaven?" Thérèse revealed, "Yes, you will go to heaven, Sister." Still, Sr. Faustina was curious and wanted to know more. "And will I be a saint?"

"Yes, you will be a saint." Thérèse said.

"But, little Therese, shall I be a saint as you are, raised to the altar?"

"Yes, you will be a saint just as I am, but you must trust in the Lord Jesus."

Sister Faustina was very happy about the blessed encounter and conversation with her favorite saint and asked St. Thérèse if her parents would go to Heaven. Saint Thérèse said they would. Sister Faustina wanted to know about her beloved brothers and sisters too. Saint Thérèse told her that they needed prayers — "to pray hard for them." We can imagine how hard Sr. Faustina began to pray for her family. God was calling her to be a great intercessor for her family and the world. In addition, saint-in-the-making Faustina learned from another saint how important it was to trust God.

Sister Faustina knew full well that all that transpired was within the confines of a dream. Still, it was very meaningful and profound to her. Indeed, three days later, St. Thérèse's prophetic words came to pass. As Sr. Faustina later recorded in her *Diary*, "[T]he difficulty was solved very easily, just as she had said. …It was a dream, but it had its significance."[50]

Staying the course

Sister Faustina's parents raised her well in the Faith and she also received great religious training at the convent, but it was sometimes very hard for her to understand the ups and downs in the spiritual life. As we know, our friend Faustina also experienced ill health and some of the sisters thought she was faking. Sister Faustina's deep desire to become holy ruffled a few feathers around the convent, as well, and some sisters shunned her for it, or even worse, made fun of her. Jesus taught Faustina the power in offering up to Him the pain and suffering she endured which He would redeem for the conversion of sinners.

Nevertheless, the young saint-in-the-making stayed the course. She strove to become a saint — something we are all called to do. In the midst of all the trails and consolations, Sr. Faustina kept moving forward with God's grace. Through it all, Jesus was transforming Sr. Faustina's heart and soul to ultimately become more like Him.

Saint Teresa of Calcutta (Mother Teresa) often said that sanctity is not the luxury for a few, but a simple duty for us all. God grants graces to all of us for the asking. He wants us to forge ahead with His grace to live a virtuous life, to love Him, and to do good for others. Because of our lives of love, we will lead countless souls to Heaven. Like Faustina, sometimes in our own lives we will be persecuted for choosing to tread a deep spiritual path. God will see us through. We must trust in His Mercy and Love.

Sister Faustina was sent to the city of Plock in the spring of 1930. She worked in the kitchen at the congregation's Guardian Angel Home. Soon after, she needed a rest. Her illness flared up and she was sent to the sisters' rest home in nearby Biala. After there a few months, Faustina returned to Plock where she helped at the bakery and store.

Grand mission revealed

Plock turned out to be the place of an extraordinary miracle and where a grand mission was revealed to the once peasant farm girl. On the evening of February 22, 1931, Sr. Faustina was in her cell when she saw something that took her breath away!

Clothed in white, Jesus suddenly appeared to Sr. Faustina. The young nun was filled with a joyful awe. She had no warning or inkling that Jesus would come to her like this. She knew His presence and remembered how He had appeared to her at the dance in Venice Park. However, His appearance was dramatically different and He was there for another reason — a huge one!

Sister Faustina later wrote every single detail in her *Diary*. She recalled the way in which, "One hand [was] raised in the gesture of blessing, the other was touching the garment at the breast." She couldn't take her eyes off of Him and saw clearly that, "From beneath the garment, slightly drawn aside at the breast, there were emanating two large rays, one red, the other pale." She wrote, "In silence I kept my gaze fixed on the Lord; my soul was struck with awe, but also with great joy."

Awestruck, Sr. Faustina stayed still, eyes fixed on Jesus and she took it all in. In a while, Jesus spoke to her. **"Paint an image according to the pattern you see, with the signature: Jesus, I trust in You. I desire that this image be venerated, first in your chapel, and [then] throughout the world."**[51] Jesus explained more:

> **"I promise that the soul that will venerate this image will not perish. I also promise victory over [its] enemies already here on earth, especially at the hour of death. I Myself will defend it as My own glory."**[52]

We can try to imagine what this must have been like for Sr. Faustina. Jesus had given to her a mammoth task — a huge undertaking — a mighty mission! How was she to paint the image Jesus asked her to paint? Would anyone believe her that Jesus had actually appeared to her in her cell? Well, whatever the case, she knew what she needed to do. She went straight to the confessional and told her confessor everything.

He told her, "Certainly, paint God's image in your soul." As soon as our friend came out of the confessional, Jesus told Sr. Faustina, **"My image already is in your soul. I desire that there be a Feast of Mercy. I want this image, which you will paint with a brush, to be solemnly blessed on the first Sunday after Easter; that Sunday is to be the Feast of Mercy."**[53] Jesus said, **"I desire that priests proclaim this great mercy of Mine towards souls of sinners. Let the sinner not be afraid to approach Me."** Jesus explained, **"The flames of mercy are burning Me — clamoring to be spent; I want to pour them out upon these souls."**[54]

Divine Mercy weighed heavily
upon her shoulders

Sister Faustina certainly learned so much from Jesus. He told her such things she never expected, but which she took straight to her heart. Why did Jesus pick her, a nun of the second choir? She might have wondered. The truth is that God always chooses the humble-hearted pure souls to deliver important messages for Him. God always equips the seemingly unequipped.

The young visionary wrote in her *Diary*, "Jesus complained to me in these words, **Distrust on the part of souls is tearing at My insides. The distrust of a chosen soul causes Me even greater pain; despite My inexhaustible love for them… Woe to the soul that abuses these** [gifts]."

Sister Faustina went to her Mother Superior Rose. She told her what happened that night and what Jesus told her and asked of her. Mother Rose told her that Jesus should give some signs so that the superiors could recognize Him more clearly. Faustina went to Jesus in prayer. She asked Him for a sign of proof so that they would know the message was all from Him. What did Jesus tell her?

He reassured her. **"I will make this all clear to the Superior by means of the graces which I will grant through this image."**[55]

Sister Faustina was happy for the reassurance from Jesus, but nothing seemed to change with regard to anyone believing her. Faustina became discouraged and wanted to run away from the interior inspirations she continually received. But God clearly let her know that He would demand of her a great many souls.[56]

She could hardly bear the pressure any longer. Sister Faustina became very exhausted because of various difficulties and because absolutely nothing was moving forward with regard to Jesus' requests of her. The weight of the task of painting the image weighed heavily upon her shoulders. She decided to meet with Fr. Andrasz before she made her perpetual vows and request that he dispense her of all her interior inspirations.

Father Andrasz heard Faustina's confession and gave his quick answer. Without hesitation, he said, "I will dispense you from nothing, Sister; it is not right for you to turn away from these interior inspirations, but you must absolutely — and I say, absolutely — speak about them to your confessor; otherwise you will go astray despite the great graces you are receiving from God."[57] We can only imagine the weight of his words upon Faustina's heart and soul.

Sister Faustina was upset because she thought she would be freed of such a difficult responsibility. But at least she had a holy priest to turn to who wasn't afraid to set the record straight. She absolutely needed to stay the course. She couldn't run away. She had tried that once before when she was younger and striving for religious life, but was confronted with her parents' refusal. It became so difficult and she thought she should shun the graces from God. However, we cannot run from difficulties. We must always pray for strength and grace and wholeheartedly trust that God will see us through.

Father Andrasz warned the young nun that she could easily go astray by turning away from these important graces and also from Jesus' instructions. Father also told her that although she had him for confessions for the time being, she needed a regular confessor who could also act as her spiritual director. God would eventually grant that request. Meanwhile, thankfully, Fr. Andrasz could help steer her in the right direction so she wouldn't go astray. He also told her to always consult with her confessor with regard to the interior inspirations.

Faustina later recorded in her *Diary*, "I was very upset by this. I thought I would get myself free from everything, and it turned out quite the opposite — an explicit command to follow the requests of Jesus. And now, still another torment, as I had no permanent confessor." In addition to Faustina being upset having no permanent confessor, it was so hard for her to open up her soul to confessors. She felt she went through "ineffable pain."

She even asked Jesus to give the special graces to someone else! She didn't know how to make use of them and didn't want to waste Heaven's time. She said, "Jesus, have mercy on me …

as You see that I am a bit of dust and completely inept" Again, we see how God uses the humble hearted.

Thankfully, before long, Jesus provided a special director named Fr. Michael Sopoćko (now Blessed Michael Sopoćko). Sister Faustina had already "met" him in an interior vision. She recorded in her *Diary*, "One day I saw him in our chapel between the altar and the confessional and suddenly heard a voice in my soul say. **This is the visible help for you on earth. He will help you carry out My will on earth**."[58]

Something to Think About

Take a few minutes to think about all that has happened in this chapter which transpired in Helena's life. There's so much to think about! Helena took a trip to Purgatory and learned about the suffering souls who need our prayers. She experienced many trials, and tribulations and humiliations.

Faustina received her veil (after reviving from fainting!), her habit, and new name, professed her vows, saw her parents, and entered the novitiate. She traveled from convent to convent, worked in the kitchen, in the bakery, at the gate, and with the wards, and ultimately received an amazing grand mission from Jesus to paint the Image of the Divine Mercy. We still don't know at this point how she will do it, but thankfully, she will finally receive a spiritual director named Fr. Michael Sopoćko who will be able to guide her.

Take a few moments to think about Sr. Faustina growing in holiness and experiencing great turmoil because of being misunderstood and after having been entrusted with so great a mission from Jesus. What would you do if you were in her shoes? Can you learn from her — a humble sincere visionary in love with Jesus? Will you ask her to pray for you?

Finally, as you might have noticed in our chapter title, our friend Faustina was considered a "nobody," supposedly, she was no one significant. She was uneducated and placed in the second choir of nuns. Yet, with God's grace and her desire to please God and serve others, dear Faustina was eventually raised to the altar as a canonized saint! She gives us great hope about our own lives! Personally, I believe that in time, she will also be proclaimed a "Doctor of the Church"!

Pray

Dear Jesus and Mary, please guide me. Jesus, I trust in You! Help me to trust You even more. Dear St. Faustina, please pray for me.

A Merciful Action

Seek to move beyond your comfort zone to reach out with kindness to someone in your life who feels insignificant.

Mary, the Mother of Mercy often sustained
Jesus' "Secretary and Apostle of Divine Mercy."
She brought comfort and reassurance to the
young nun, as well as important instructions.

6

Mother Mary in Her Life

Jesus continued to guide His special soul through words of instruction from the holy men and women whom He placed in her life, as well as His own directions and those of His Mother Mary.

One of Faustina's confessors told her, "Sister, God is preparing many special graces for you, but try to make your life as clear as crystal before the Lord, paying no attention to what anyone else thinks about you. Let God suffice; He alone."[59] This is wise counsel we can all apply to our lives.

Another time, Sr. Faustina was told by a Fr. Theodore, "Act in such a way that all those who come in contact with you will go away joyful. Sow happiness about you because you have received much from God; give, then, generously to others. They should take leave of you with their hearts filled with joy, even if they have no more than touched the hem of your garment. Keep well in mind the words I am telling you right now." Later on, Father told her, "Let God push your boat out into the deep waters, towards the unfathomable depths of the interior life."

Allowing God to push her boat out into deep waters meant Sr. Faustina prayed for the graces to stay the course and the courage to step out in Faith — to push beyond her comfort zone to totally trust in God's holy will for her life. She knew she couldn't do it on her own strength. Young Faustina continued to prayerfully move forward with God's grace. At times, the journey seemed to her as if she were floating along on tranquil waters under sunny skies as God gently guided her boat. These times, she felt His consolations. Most times, though, the saint-in-the-making's spiritual work was utterly arduous, like rowing her little boat with all her might against fierce killer waves, and tempestuous wind in her face, while out on a stormy sea.

Towards the end of her novitiate, Sr. Faustina received another important instruction. This time from her Mother directress, who told her, "Sister, let simplicity and humility be the characteristic traits of your soul. Go through life like a little child, always trusting, always full of simplicity and humility, content with everything, happy in every circumstance. There, where others fear, you will pass calmly along, thanks to this simplicity and humility. Remember this, Sister, for your whole life: as waters flow from the mountains down into the valleys, so, too, do God's graces flow only into humble souls."[60]

Sister Faustina continued to listen well to her superior's counsel and prayed earnestly to carry out the instructions while striving to trust God with all her heart.

Mother Mary on the journey

We recall that when Jesus was being crucified on the Cross for our sins, He gave us the eminent gift of His own Mother. He wants us to get to know His dear Mother more intimately. Mother Mary was an integral part of Sr. Faustina's spiritual journey. The great Mother of God guided and sustained Sr. Faustina in her mission. The Blessed Mother always reinforced the teachings the young nun received from Jesus.

In fact, the Blessed Mother told Faustina, "*I gave the Savior to the world; as for you, you have to speak to the world about His great mercy and prepare the world for the Second Coming of Him who will come, not as a merciful Savior, but as a just Judge. Oh, how terrible is that day!*"[61] These were certainly profound and stirring words which Sr. Faustina needed to heed.

For a moment, let's step back to the beginning — back home in Głogowiec, Lodz. In her cradle — her father's singing of morning hymns to Mary (*The Little Office of the Immaculate Conception*) imbued baby Helena's ears. Sister Faustina was raised with the sure knowledge that the Mother of God was very much a part of her life.

As a young girl, Sr. Faustina had developed a strong devotion to Mary. Sister Faustina's family together prayed many prayers to Mary including The Litany of Loreto every day during summer months, gathered around a little shrine hanging on the pear tree in front of their home. In October, the family prayed the Rosary together each day.

When Sr. Faustina ran off to join a convent, she was certain of what she needed to do but felt sorrowful over the fact that her parents would be displeased. She surely needed a mother to help her when feeling so out of sorts.

Earlier, we learned that Sister Faustina did not hesitate to cry out to her Mother in Heaven the moment she felt lost and confused upon arriving in the big city of Warsaw. She was certainly frightened and realized she knew not a soul there. Jesus had instructed her to go there and enter a convent.

Not knowing how to do so, Faustina begged the Blessed Virgin, "Mary, lead me, guide me."[62]

Later on, she wrote in her *Diary*, "Immediately I heard these words within me telling me to leave the town and to go to a nearby village where I would find a safe lodging for the night. I did so and found, in fact, that everything was just as the Mother of God told me."[63]

The Blessed Mother certainly came through for her daughter Faustina. Faustina's holy journey to the convent had begun with Jesus' and Mary's instructions. Interestingly, Helena was guided by them to the convent of the Congregation of the Sisters of Our Lady of Mercy. It was there that her devotion to her Mother in Heaven advanced considerably, especially since the Congregation's main Patroness is Our Lady of Mercy.

Early in the religious life, six hours spent before the image of the Black Madonna at the shrine in Czestochowa, Poland turned out to be an important part of Faustina's spiritual journey. Sister Faustina was so steeped in prayer, she lost track of time and another sister had to fetch her from the shrine in order for her to have a quick meal and to run off to catch a train. Sister Faustina later revealed that the Blessed Mother spoke much and very deeply to her heart during those long prayerful hours.

When Sr. Faustina professed her perpetual vows, she made three requests to Jesus, telling Him she knew in her heart He wouldn't refuse her.[64] She also prayed a special prayer to her Mother in Heaven. She, in a sense, referred to Mary as her mother-in-law, but also her dearest Mother. She prayed:

> Mother of God, Most Holy Mary, my Mother, You are my Mother in a special way now because Your beloved Son is my Bridegroom, and thus we are both Your children. For Your Son's sake, You have to love me. O Mary, my dearest Mother, guide my spiritual life in such a way that it will please Your Son.[65]

Mary's visits to Faustina

Mary, the Mother of Mercy often sustained Jesus' "Secretary and Apostle of Divine Mercy." She brought comfort and reassurance to the young nun, as well as important instructions. At times, she did so by appearing to Sr. Faustina.

Mary often visited Sr. Faustina accompanied by her Son and also made known that she is the one who leads us to Jesus. One time the Blessed Mother visited the young visionary with St. Joseph and Baby Jesus and she gave Faustina a precious and surprising gift. It was on February 2, 1936. Sister Faustina was having trouble meditating and praying that day because her mind was filled with "absurd thoughts." However, when she was at Mass, she experienced a "strange silence and joy" that filled her heart.

> Just then, I saw Our Lady with the Infant Jesus, and the Holy Old Man [St. Joseph] standing behind them. The most holy Mother said to me, *Take My Dearest Treasure*, and She handed me the Infant Jesus. When I took then Infant Jesus in my arms, the Mother of God and Saint Joseph disappeared. I was left alone with the Infant Jesus.[66]

Wow! Can we even imagine the great gift this mystical experience must have been for Sr. Faustina? With the Infant Jesus in her arms, Sr. Faustina said to Him, "I know that You are my Lord and Creator even though You are so tiny." Just then, Jesus stretched His little arms out towards Faustina and looked straight at her with a smile. Filled with joy, Sr. Faustina was immensely awestruck. Jesus, then disappeared and it was time for Holy Communion. Sister Faustina's soul was deeply moved as she walked forward with the other sisters to receive Jesus in the Eucharist.

Still, another great gift was about to be given to the saint-in-the-making. After receiving Holy Communion, Sr. Faustina heard these words: **"I am in your heart, I whom you had in your arms."** Sister Faustina immediately pleaded with Jesus to give special help to Fr. Sopoćko, who was experiencing great difficulties due to the message and mission of Divine Mercy. Jesus told the young mystic, **"As you ask, so shall it be, but his merit will not be lessened."** Sister Faustina was overjoyed at Jesus' words. She later recalled in her *Diary* what was on her heart.

She wrote, "God is so good and merciful; God grants everything that we ask of Him with trust."[67] We should take her wise words to our own hearts. God will indeed grant everything that we ask for with great trust in Him — assuming, of course, that what we are asking for is in full accord with His will. With regard to praying the Divine Mercy Chaplet, Jesus Himself tells us, **"Through this Chaplet you will obtain everything, if what you ask for is according to My will."**[68]

One night, during Sr. Faustina's novitiate when she was enduring a painful bout of suffering, Our Lady came to the rescue. Sister Faustina's unrelenting suffering suddenly melted away as she was overcome with joy upon seeing Our Lady appearing to her to comfort her in her suffering. The Blessed Mother was holding the Infant Jesus in her arms. As soon as Faustina saw beautiful Mary, she asked her a question. "Mary, my Mother, do you know how terribly I suffer?"

That evening, the Blessed Mother didn't hesitate to answer Faustina. She said, *"I know how much you suffer, but do not be afraid. I share with you your suffering, and I shall always do so."*[69] Our Lady smiled warmly at St. Faustina and then disappeared. Sister Faustina received immediate graces and strength, and courage was immediately restored in her soul. Even so, Faustina's suffering came back quickly.

Another time, Our Lady appeared to Sr. Faustina in her cell when she was unable to attend holy Mass. It was the feast of the Assumption of Mary and this made it particularly painful for the young novice, who was told by her doctor that she was not allowed out of her room due to weaknesses from her illness. Sister Faustina wanted to celebrate her holy Mother in Heaven with the others at Mass, but instead, she prayed fervently by herself in her cell.

Suddenly, the Mother of God appeared to her. Sister Faustina later recalled in her *Diary* that Mary was "unspeakably beautiful." Mary had a special mission for the young visionary and would ask her to pray a particular intercessory novena, offering herself to God:

> "*My daughter, what I demand from you is prayer, prayer, and once again prayer, for the world and especially for your country. For nine days receive Holy Communion in atonement and unite yourself closely to the Holy Sacrifice of the Mass. During these nine days you will stand before God as an offering; always and everywhere, at all times and places, day or night, whenever you wake up, pray in the spirit. In spirit, one can always remain in prayer.*"[70]

Another time, Sr. Faustina's confessor asked her for prayers for a special intention. Sister Faustina began a novena to the Mother of God. In response to her fervent novena, the Mother of God came to the young nun with special words that touched her heart.

Sister Faustina later recorded the prayer experience in her *Diary*:

> I began a novena to the Mother of God. This novena consisted in the prayer, "Hail, Holy Queen," recited nine times. Toward the end of the novena I saw the Mother of God with the Infant Jesus in Her arms, and I also saw my confessor kneeling at Her feet and talking with Her. I did not understand what he was

saying to Her, because I was busy talking with the Infant Jesus, who came down from His Mother's arms and approached me. I could not stop wondering at His beauty. I heard a few of the words that the Mother of God spoke to him [i.e., my confessor] but not everything. The words were: *I am not only the Queen of Heaven, but also the Mother of Mercy and your Mother.* And at that moment She stretched out her right hand, in which She was clasping her mantle, and She covered the priest with it. At that moment, the vision vanished.[71]

Mother Mary's profound and poignant words to Sr. Faustina can be considered a special message that we can take to our own hearts: "I am not only the Queen of Heaven, but also the Mother of Mercy and your Mother." Mary is our Mother. As I briefly touched upon earlier, but bears a reminder here, Mary was gifted to us by her Son Jesus when He was hanging from the Cross. He called down to His disciple John, "Here is your mother." He was also speaking to all of His disciples down to the end of time, telling us all that His own Mother Mary had become our Mother! He gifted us with our loving Mother Mary, full of compassion for us and totally attuned to the thoughts of God, completely imbued with the Word of God.

Mother of Mercy

Sister Faustina knew that the Mother of God, having been preserved from the stain of original sin, was endowed with the fullness of grace and had obtained Mercy to the very highest degree. The young Jewish Mary, by the power of the Holy Spirit had become the Mother of God's Son, Who resided and was nourished in her own Immaculate womb, which became His first tabernacle.

By the workings of the Holy Spirit, Mother Mary gave Mercy Incarnate (Jesus) to the whole world. Indeed, Mary has the deepest knowledge of God's great mystery. Mary shared in her Son's messianic mission and stood at the foot of her Son's Cross. She witnessed the shedding of His Blood while He also forgave those who were putting Him to death. She knew full well why Jesus was willing to die for our salvation. He is a God of unfathomable Mercy and Love.

Our friend Faustina also knew that God grants mercy through Mary. Being a nun in the Congregation of Our Lady of Mercy, Sr. Faustina learned to continuously call upon Our Lady of Mercy for help to do the will of God. On August 5, 1935, the Feast of Our Lady of Mercy, Mary appeared to Faustina. Sister Faustina had been struggling through her prayers that day and was experiencing various doubts. She had prayerfully prepared well for this feast, but it seemed the evil one was tormenting and distracting her with many struggles.

Sister Faustina quickly turned to Mary in prayer, telling her of her difficulties. Later on, Faustina recorded the experience in her *Diary:*

> Then I saw the Blessed Virgin, unspeakably beautiful. She came down from the altar to my kneeler, held me close to herself and said to me, *I am Mother to you all, thanks to the unfathomable mercy of God. Most pleasing to Me is that soul which faithfully carries out the will of God.* She gave me to understand that I had faithfully fulfilled the will of God and had thus found favor in His eyes. *Be courageous. Do not fear apparent obstacles, but fix your gaze upon the Passion of My Son, and in this way you will be victorious.*[72]

Can we even imagine being hugged by Mother Mary? And this was not the only time. Mary held Faustina close and communicated extraordinarily good news to the young nun. She had found favor with Jesus! Faustina was also told that she was pleasing to her Mother! How amazing she must have felt. This beautiful consolation gave the young nun strength for the continual arduous journey in carrying out her special mission to propagate the message of Divine Mercy.

The Blessed Virgin's message to Sr. Faustina to be courageous and not fear, but instead, meditate upon Jesus' Passion to become victorious, speaks to our hearts, as well. Being victorious means to be able to rise above the obstacles and struggles in life with God's grace to achieve following God's holy will, which will help our own soul and the souls of others. In Sr. Faustina's case, being victorious had everything to do with carrying out the mission of Divine Mercy.

Sister Faustina deeply loved her Heavenly Mother. One time, during the Congregation's nine-day novena, Sr. Faustina wanted to greatly please Mary and give special honor to her, so she prayed one thousand Hail Mary's on each of the days! On the actual feast day, the Virgin Mary came to Sr. Faustina at Mass. She smiled at Sr. Faustina and told her that, at God's command, the Blessed Virgin Mary was to be in a special and exclusive way Sr. Faustina's mother and told her she desired that Sr. Faustina would be, in a special way, her child.

In her prayer of Adoration for "God of Mercy," Sr. Faustina speaks about Mary, Mother of Mercy. We can take a moment to mediate upon Faustina's wise reflection:

> Unfathomable and incomprehensible in Your mercy,
> For love of us You take on flesh
> From the Immaculate Virgin, ever untouched by sin,
> Because You have willed it so from all ages.
>
> The Blessed Virgin, that Snow-White Lily,
> Is first to praise the omnipotence of Your mercy.
> Her pure heart opens with love for the coming of the Word;
>
> She believes the words of God's messenger and is confirmed in trust. …
>
> To give worthy praise to the Lord's mercy,
> We unite ourselves with Your Immaculate Mother,
> For then our hymn will be more pleasing to You,
> Because She is chosen from among men and angels
>
> Through Her, as through a pure crystal …
> streams of grace flowed down upon us.[73]

Merciful Mary even shared with her daughter Faustina the "anxious concern" she felt because of her Son Jesus. Saint Faustina recalled the experience in her *Diary* on Christmas Eve, 1937, doing her best to express it in her notebook.

> After Holy Communion, the Mother of God gave me to experience the anxious concern she had in her heart because of the Son of God. But this anxiety was permeated with such fragrance of abandonment to the will of God that I should call it rather a delight than an anxiety. I understood how my soul ought to accept the will of God in all things. It is a pity I cannot write this the way I experienced it. My soul was plunged in deep recollection all day long. Nothing could tear me away from this recollection, neither duties, nor the business I had with lay people.[74]

Imagine receiving the gift of experiencing what our Mother in Heaven felt? We can prayerfully meditate upon St. Faustina's words above and learn about abandonment to God's will from the humble mystic and the great Mother of God.

Rosary

Sister Faustina was very dedicated to praying the holy Rosary and learned to love it as a child. Praying the Rosary for Faustina was for her as natural as breathing. She even prayed the five decades of the Rosary on Saturdays with her arms outstretched (to resemble Jesus on the Cross) as a little mortification. Try that some time. It's not so easy! On April 25, 1933, included in a list of other mortifications, Faustina wrote: "On Saturday, to say five decades of the Rosary with outstretched arms."[75]

Once when Sr. Faustina was working in the garden, her guardian angel summoned her to pray for the dying and St. Faustina immediately began to pray the Rosary and asked the gardeners to pray along with her.[76]

On October 3, 1936, Sr. Faustina suddenly saw a ciborium with the Blessed Sacrament during her prayers of the Rosary. She later wrote in her *Diary*, "The ciborium was uncovered and quite filled with hosts. From the ciborium came a voice: **These hosts have been received by souls converted through your prayer and suffering.** At this point, I felt God's presence as a child would; I felt strangely like a child."[77]

One time she wrote in her *Diary* about the power of the Rosary over Satan and demons tormenting her. In addition, she shared some powerful words from Jesus, Who explained the evil one's hatred towards her.

She wrote:

> But towards evening I felt very exhausted and could not make my Holy Hour, so I asked Mother Superior to allow me to go to bed early. I fell asleep as soon as I lay down, but at about eleven o'clock Satan shook my bed. I awoke instantly, and I started to pray peacefully to my Guardian Angel. Then I saw the souls who were doing penance in purgatory. They appeared like shadows, and among them I saw many demons. One of these tried to vex me; taking the form of a cat, he kept throwing himself onto my bed and on my feet, and he was quite heavy, as if [weighing] a ton. I kept praying the rosary all the while, and toward dawn these beings vanished, and I was able to get some sleep. When I entered the chapel in the morning I heard a voice in my soul, **You are united to Me; fear nothing. But know, my child, that Satan hates you; he hates every soul, but he burns with a particular hatred for you, because you have snatched so many souls from his dominion.**[78]

Eventually, Sr. Faustina would express, "[It was Our Lady who] taught me how to love God interiorly and also how to carry out His holy will in all things. O Mary, You are my joy, because through You God descended to earth [and] into my heart."[79]

Sister Faustina learned so much from her Mother in Heaven, who was completely inseparable from her Son Jesus and His mission of Divine Mercy. Faustina noted in her *Dairy,*

"The humility and love of the Immaculate Virgin penetrated my soul. The more I imitate the Mother of God, the more deeply I get to know God."[80] Saint Faustina teaches and inspires us to imitate Mary's virtues and we can become closer to God.

Next, we are going to discuss the fascinating subject of dead souls contacting Sr. Faustina. But first, take a few moments to prayerfully ponder a few things.

 ## Something to Think About

Take a moment to think about what you've learned in this chapter. Remember, Sr. Faustina's Mother directress' instructions: "[L]et simplicity and humility be the characteristic traits of your soul. Go through life like a little child, always trusting, always full of simplicity and humility, content with everything, happy in every circumstance. There, where others fear, you will pass calmly along, thanks to this simplicity and humility ..." Pray to be like this, as well.

In addition, Fr. Theodore instructed Sr. Faustina: "Act in such a way that all those who come in contact with you will go away joyful. Sow happiness ... give, then, generously to others ... Let God push your boat out into deep waters, towards the unfathomable depths of the interior life." Can you pray for the graces from God to also strive for this?

Finally, do you pray to Mother Mary on a regular basis? Do you pray the Rosary? Mother Mary always helps us to stay on the holy road to Heaven. She will grant many graces to us for the asking. Mary also knows our sorrows and struggles. She has endured the same, and worse.

We should never be afraid to approach Mary with anything. Remember, Mary was human like us — she needed to move her will — to decide to pray — to choose to do good. Mary awaits our greetings and conversations with her. She knows our hearts. She shows us how to really love and follow God's holy will. Mary shows us how to be spiritually beautiful and humble for our Lord. We need to turn to Mary often, praying to emulate her virtues.

One time when I was going through a precarious pregnancy, St. Teresa of Calcutta (Mother Teresa) whom I knew at that time, told me to pray simply to Mother Mary whenever in need. She said to pray, "Mary, Mother of Jesus, be Mother to me now." We all need Mother Mary. We can pray many prayers and novenas to her, as well as Rosaries. However, we can also pray simply to her and ask her to be our Mother. She will always help us!

 Pray

Dear Jesus and Mary, please guide me. Mary, Mother of Jesus, be Mother to me now. Jesus, I trust in You! Dear St. Faustina, please pray for me.

 A Merciful Action

Endeavor to help someone learn more about the Blessed Mother. Pray to Mary and ask her to help you.

Sister Faustina was learning about the needs
of the Holy Souls in Purgatory, and that even
religious souls need our prayers.

7

Dead Souls Sought Her Help

The Catholic Church teaches in her *Catechism*, "All who die in God's grace and friendship, but still imperfectly purified, are indeed assured of their eternal salvation; but after death they undergo purification, so as to achieve the holiness necessary to enter the joy of heaven." (*CCC*, 1030)

Purgatory is much more a mercy than a punishment. A Holy Soul in Purgatory desires to be perfect before God. Because it does, the Holy Soul spends a period of time in Purgatory before finally seeing God face-to-face in Heaven for all eternity.

When Helena was searching for a convent to enter, she had no idea then that praying for the Holy Souls in Purgatory would become such an important part of her mission in religious life. Jesus initially revealed the holy place of purification to her by having Helena's guardian angel escort the young nun to Purgatory early in her religious life. What a way to start out!

Helena came to know how very important it was to pray for the Holy Souls in Purgatory. In fact, when she professed her perpetual vows as a nun, she did not forget about the Holy Souls. On the day of her profession of vows, she asked Jesus for three main requests. She told her Lord and Savior, "Jesus, I know that today You will refuse me nothing."

Sister Faustina asked help for many people, including her parents and the wards she cared for, for the clergy, her confessors, superiors, for the salvation of souls, as well as other important requests. She did not hesitate to ask for help for the Holy Souls in Purgatory and was very bold in how she worded her request.

The undaunted mystic said, "I plead with You for the souls that are most in need of prayer. I plead for the dying; be merciful to them." Now, here's her almost outlandish request: "I also beg You, Jesus, to free all souls from purgatory."[81] She wanted every single Holy Soul out of Purgatory to immediately enjoy the rewards of everlasting life in Heaven!

Can we be so caring about the Holy Souls?

We discussed earlier about Helena's experience of Purgatory, seeing the souls suffer, learning their greatest suffering, and seeing the Blessed Mother ("The Star of the Sea") bring refreshment to the Holy Souls.

Remember, when Helena left Purgatory, ushered out by her Guardian Angel, she heard Jesus say, **"My mercy does not want this, but justice demands it."** And Helena wrote in her *Diary*, "Since that time, I am in closer communion with the suffering souls."[82]

With that little backdrop under our belts, in this chapter, we will delve deeper into just how and when Sr. Faustina prayed for the holy souls and about the mysterious souls that came to visit her!

Surprising night visitors!

We learned earlier that something incredible happened when Sr. Faustina arrived in Warsaw on January 23, 1926 to finish out her postulancy period. I hinted at it earlier. Well, on that very day, a young sister was dying at the convent. It was 29-year-old Henryka Losinska, a shoemaker in the second choir. We don't know the reason for her dying at such a young age.

Several days after Sr. Henryka had passed away, Faustina received a visit from the dead sister. Sister Henryka came to Helena in spirit with a big request and because she did, Helena soon learned the power of prayer in aiding the Holy Souls in Purgatory.

Here's what happened: Sister Henryka begged a favor from Sr. Faustina. She appeared to her and asked that Faustina tell Mother Malgorzata Gimbutt (the Directress of novices at that time) that she, the deceased, would like Fr. Stanislaus Rospond (her director, and later a bishop) to offer up one Mass and three ejaculatory (quick) prayers for her.

At first, Sr. Faustina agreed, but then later feared it might have been a dream and decided not to go to the Mother Directress. Sister Faustina later wrote about it in her *Diary*.

> The following night the same thing was repeated more clearly; I had no more doubt. Still, in the morning I decided not to tell the Directress about it unless I saw her [Sister Henry] during the day. At once I ran into her in the corridor. She reproached me for not having gone immediately, and a great uneasiness filled my soul. So I went immediately to Mother Directress and told her everything that had happened to me. Mother responded that she would take care of the matter. At once peace reigned in my soul, and on the third day this sister came to me and said, "May God repay you."[83]

Sister Faustina was learning about the needs of the Holy Souls in Purgatory, and that even religious souls need our prayers.

Another time, one night, a Sister from the first choir visited Faustina. She had died two months prior to the visit.

Sister Faustina recalled:

> I saw her in a terrible condition, all in flames with her face painfully distorted. This lasted only a short time, and then she disappeared. A shudder went through my soul because I did not know whether she was suffering in purgatory or in hell. Nevertheless, I redoubled my prayers for her. The next night she came again, but I saw her in an even more horrible state, in the midst of flames which were even more intense, and despair was written all over her face. I was astonished to see her in a worse condition after the prayers I had offered for her, and I asked, "Haven't my prayers helped you?" She answered that my prayers had not helped her and that nothing would help her. I said to her, "And the prayers which the whole community has offered for you, have they not been any help to you?" She said no, that these prayers had helped some other souls.

I replied, "If my prayers are not helping you, Sister, please stop coming to me." She disappeared at once. Despite this, I kept on praying.[84]

Sometime later on, the deceased Sister returned one night to Sr. Faustina, who was happy to see that her appearance had changed. No more flames and her face was radiant — her eyes beamed with joy. The deceased Sister complimented Faustina, telling her that she had a "true love" for her neighbor.

She also encouraged Faustina to continue her prayers for the Holy Souls in Purgatory telling her that many souls had profited from her prayers. Good thing Faustina didn't give up praying for them when the sister previously told her that her prayers had not helped her. The deceased Sister told Sr. Faustina that she herself would leave Purgatory very soon. Sister Faustina marveled and wrote in her *Diary*: "How astounding are the decrees of God!"[85]

Can we even imagine Sr. Faustina's surprise when deceased sisters came to her for prayers? Sister Faustina recalled another deceased sister in need of prayers.

When Sister Dominic died at about one o'clock in the night, she came to me and gave me to know that she was dead. I prayed fervently for her. In the morning, the sisters told me that she was no longer alive, and I replied that I knew, because she had visited me. The sister infirmarian [Sister Chrysostom] asked me to help dress her. And then when I was alone with her, the Lord gave me to know that she was still suffering in purgatory. I redoubled my prayers for her. However, despite the zeal with which I always pray for our deceased sisters, I got mixed up as regards the days, and instead of offering three days of prayer, as the rule directs us to do, by mistake I offered only two days. On the fourth day, she gave me to know that I still owed her prayers, and that she was in need of them. I immediately formed the intention of offering the whole day for her, and not just that day but much more, as love of neighbor dictated to me.[86]

If only we could be so generous with our prayers, perhaps Purgatory would be empty!

The soul of a young lady came to Sr. Faustina one night and made it known that she needed her prayer. Sister Faustina prayed for a while but the spirit did not leave her. She finally thought to tell the spirit, "If you are a good spirit, leave me in peace, and the indulgences I will gain tomorrow will be for you."[87] The spirit left the cell immediately and Sr. Faustina recognized that the spirit was in Purgatory.

Sister Faustina was visited frequently by the souls in need of help. She prayed the Divine Mercy Chaplet for them, as well as other prayers. She was often able to confirm what was going on by looking at her watch when the souls came to her and sometimes it was before their deaths.

Sister Faustina noted in her *Diary,* "This is how I have verified the exact time: I have a watch, and I look to see what time it is. On the following day, when they tell me about that person's death, I ask them about the time, and it exactly corresponds, as does the length of the person's last agony. They say to me, 'Such and such a person died today, but she passed away quickly and peacefully.' It sometimes happens that the dying person is in the second or third building away, yet for the spirit, space does not exist. It sometimes happens that I know about a death occurring several hundred kilometers away."[88]

Communion of Saints

Saint Faustina was very generous with her prayers and offerings for the Holy Souls in Purgatory. In her communing with the Holy Souls, she also learned quite a bit. After one particular visit, Faustina made note of how she came to understand more fully about the importance of the Communion of Saints. She also received an embrace from a Sister in Heaven!

Here's what happened: One evening, a deceased Sister appeared once again to Sr. Faustina. She had visited a few times prior to that evening. The first time she came to Faustina's cell, the nun was experiencing great suffering. Over time, the sufferings began to diminish. This evening, she was "radiant with happiness," and communicated to Faustina that she was now in Heaven. However, she had an important message for her. Sister Faustina later wrote it in her *Diary*.

> She told me that God had tried our house with tribulation because Mother General [Michael] had given in to doubts, not believing what I had said about this soul. And further, as a sign that she only now was in heaven, God would bless our house. Then she came closer to me, embraced me sincerely and said, "I must go now." I understood how closely the three stages of a soul's life are bound together; that is to say, life on earth, in purgatory and in heaven [the Communion of Saints].[89]

Each and every one of us is an important member of the Communion of Saints. We are all connected to one another. We are all members of Christ. References to this belief can be traced back as far as the fourth century. The term Communion of Saints is in our Apostle's Creed.

Our earthly life is gifted to us to work out our eternal salvation. Each day, we are making our journey to Heaven. This branch of the Communion of Saints on earth is called the Church Militant. The Holy Souls in Purgatory are being purified so that they can go to Heaven and are called the Church Penitent or Church Suffering. The souls already in Heaven are called the Church Triumphant.

Each branch of the Communion of Saints helps one another on the spiritual journey. The saints in Heaven pray for us — they intercede for us so that we may get to Heaven one day. We can ask them for their prayers. The saints in Heaven and we on Earth can pray for the Holy Souls in Purgatory. The Holy Souls can pray for us here on Earth, but can no longer pray for themselves. We can have Masses said for them and pray for them to get to Heaven soon.

Experiencing Purgatory

On the evening of July 9, 1937, a deceased sister came to visit Sr. Faustina. She requested a day of fasting from her and that she offer all of her spiritual exercises of that day for her. Sister Faustina agreed to help her in that way. But she did not know when she agreed that the good Lord was going to allow her to actually experience a taste of what a Holy Soul in Purgatory goes through in their longing for God.

She explained in her *Diary*:

> From early morning on the following day, I offered everything for her intention. During Holy Mass, I had a brief experience of her torment. I experienced such intense hunger for God that I seemed to be dying of the desire to become united with Him. This lasted only a short time, but I understood what the longing of the souls in purgatory was like.
>
> Immediately after Holy Mass, I asked Mother Superior's permission to fast, but I did not receive it because of my illness. When I entered the chapel, I heard these words: "If you had fasted, Sister, I would not have gotten relief until the evening, but for the sake of your obedience, which prevented you from fasting, I obtained this relief at once. Obedience has great power." After these words I heard: "May God reward you."[90]

Jesus had requested of Sr. Faustina, "**Enter into purgatory often, because they need you there**." Faustina immediately answered her Lord Jesus, "O my Jesus, I understand the meaning of these words which you are speaking to me, but first let me enter the treasury of Your mercy."[91]

Another time, Sr. Faustina was actually told by Jesus that she herself was deserving of one day in Purgatory! She had been summoned to the judgment seat of God! Faustina was alone before God and Jesus appeared as He did in the Passion. So much happened in those mysterious moments. I'll let Faustina tell you.

After a moment, His wounds disappeared except for five, those in His hands, His feet and His side. Suddenly I saw the complete condition of my soul as God sees it. I could clearly see all that is displeasing to God. I did not know that even the smallest transgressions will have to be accounted for. What a moment! Who can describe it? To stand before the Thrice-Holy God![92]

> Then, Jesus asked Faustina, **"Who are you?"**
> She answered, "I am Your servant, Lord."
> Jesus told her, **"You are guilty of one day of fire in purgatory."**

Sister Faustina wanted to throw herself "immediately into the flames of purgatory." But Jesus stopped her and said, **"Which do you prefer, suffer now for one day in purgatory or for a short while on earth?"**

Faustina replied, "Jesus, I want to suffer in purgatory, and I want to suffer also the greatest pains on earth, even if it were until the end of the world."

Jesus said, **"One** [of the two] **is enough; you will go back to earth, and there you will suffer much, but not for long; you will accomplish My will and My desires, and a faithful servant of Mine will help you to do this."**

Then, the Lord Jesus called her to take comfort in His Sacred heart. **"Now, rest your head on My bosom, on My heart, and draw from it strength and power for these sufferings because you will find neither relief nor help nor comfort anywhere else. Know that you will have much, much to suffer, but don't let this frighten you; I am with you."**[93]

Can we even imagine? And if dear Faustina, so pure, and so humble deserved a day in Purgatory, what might we deserve? Whatever it would be, let us take comfort in Jesus' words of consolation to His dear Faustina, His Secretary and Apostle of Divine Mercy. We too, can strive to draw near to Jesus' Sacred Heart for relief when we are weary or suffering.

Jesus asks us to pray for souls

One time, Jesus gave Faustina the words for a nine-day Novena of prayer to Divine Mercy. He instructed Faustina to write down the intentions for the nine-day novena that would begin on Good Friday. You will see the entire Divine Mercy Novena in the Appendix of prayers in the back of this book. For now, I will share just the part that pertains to Purgatory.

First, Jesus began:

> **I desire that during these nine days you bring souls to the fount of My mercy, that they may draw therefrom strength and refreshment and whatever grace they need in the hardships of life, and especially, at the hour of death. On each day you will bring to My Heart a different group of souls, and you will immerse them in this ocean of My mercy, and I will bring all these souls into the house of My Father. You will do this in this life and in the next. I will deny nothing to any soul whom you will bring to the fount of My mercy. On each day you will beg My Father, on the strength of My bitter Passion, for graces for these souls.**[94]

The eighth day would be for the Holy Souls in Purgatory:

> **Today bring to Me the souls who are in the prison of Purgatory, and immerse them in the abyss of My mercy. Let the torrents of My Blood cool down their scorching flames. All these souls are greatly loved by Me. They are making retribution to My justice. It is in your power to bring them relief. Draw all the indulgences from the treasury of My Church and offer them on their behalf. Oh, if you only knew the torments they suffer, you would continually offer for them the alms of the spirit and pay off their debt to My justice.**[95]

Pray for the dying

In addition to praying for the deceased, St. Faustina prayed for the dying. The Holy Souls in Purgatory need prayerful help, but so do the souls of the dying. Souls who were dying also came to Sr. Faustina. And our friend Faustina knew at those times she was to pray for the dying.

For instance, one time out in the garden, Sr. Faustina's guardian angel told her to pray for the dying and so she asked the gardeners that were with her to also pray. I mentioned earlier that they prayed a Rosary for them and various other prayers.

Sister Faustina wrote in her *Diary*:

> After the prayers, the wards began to chat gayly among themselves. In spite of the noise they were making, I heard these words in my soul: "Pray for me!" But as I could not understand these words very well, I moved a few steps away from the wards, trying to think who it could be who was asking me to pray.

She then heard the words: "I am Sister ...." This sister was in Warsaw while Faustina was in Vilnius.

"Pray for me until I tell you to stop. I am dying." The sister asked Faustina.

Sister Faustina later recorded in her *Diary*, "Immediately, I began to pray fervently for her, [addressing myself] to the expiring Heart of Jesus." Faustina continued prayers because the Sister did not yet say to stop.

"I kept praying from three [o'clock] until five. At five, I heard the words: "Thank you!" and I understood that she had died." However, kind Faustina continued to pray fervently for her soul during Holy Mass on the following day.

"In the afternoon, a postcard came saying that Sister ... had died at such and such a time. I understood that it was at the same hour when she had said to me, 'Pray for me.'"[96]

One day, Sr. Faustina suffered with the Lord's Passion in her body more than at other times. She believed it was for the sake of a dying soul.[97] We too, should pray for the graces to desire to aid the Holy Souls in Purgatory and dying souls. They need our prayers. They will also pray for us. There are many other mentions in the *Diary* of St. Faustina praying for the Holy Souls in Purgatory and for the dying.

 ## Something to Think About

Take a moment to think about what you've learned in this chapter. Saint Faustina is an excellent example of someone who puts others before herself and who is attentive to the will of God. She knew that Jesus called her to sacrifice her time to pray extra prayers for the Holy Souls in Purgatory, as well as for those who are dying and need prayerful help so that they will choose to turn to God in their last moments.

Ask St. Faustina to intercede for you for the graces to have a generous heart in your willingness to pray for others, especially for the Holy Souls in Purgatory who depend upon the prayers of others, as well as for the dying so that they will receive the prayerful help needed at such a critical time.

 ## Pray

Dear Jesus and Mary, please guide me. Help me to be more generous with my prayers for all in need, especially the Holy Souls in Purgatory and the dying. Jesus, I trust in You! Dear St. Faustina, please pray for me.

 ## A Merciful Action

Carve out time to pray for the Holy Souls in Purgatory and for the dying that they would turn to God before they die.

"Then I saw one of the seven spirits near me, radiant as at other times, under a form of light. I constantly saw him beside me when I was riding on the train. I saw an angel standing on every church we passed, but surrounded by a light which was paler than that of the spirit who was accompanying me on the journey, and each of these spirits who were guarding the churches bowed his head to the spirit who was near me" (*Diary*, 630).

8

Angels and Demons in St. Faustina's life

We are surrounded by the invisible world of angels! Because we cannot see them, we might not think about them or even realize that they actually exist and are nearby for our assistance. Yet, the world of angels has existed since the dawn of creation!

God created the angels before He created the physical universe, including mankind. God certainly wants us to know about the angels and to pray to them for help on our journey through life. Angels are God's special messengers, mentioned in both the Old and New Testaments. The angels shouted for joy when God created the earth (Job 38:4, 7). We don't worship angels. We actually worship God along with the angels.

The *Catechism* teaches, "The Church venerates the angels who help her on her earthly pilgrimage and protect every human being." (352) Saint Thomas Aquinas stated, "The angels work together for the benefit of us all." (350)

Each one of us is immensely blessed to be gifted by God with a special angel companion as a holy guide throughout our lives. That would be our Guardian Angel. At each and every Catholic Mass, we are invited to join the angels in singing of the glory of God!

We learn in Hebrews 1:14, "Are not all angels spirits in the divine service, sent to serve for the sake of those who are to inherit salvation?" Some of the saints, such as St. Padre Pio and St. Gemma Galgani had direct experiences with angels. Saint Faustina was one such saint. Amazingly, holy angels accompanied St. Faustina on her trips and she could actually see the angels! She could even hear them singing at times.

Faustina noted in her *Diary,* "Today is the renewal; that is, the profession of vows in the course of a solemn celebration. As the sisters were making their vows, I heard angels singing in various tones. 'Holy, Holy, Holy,' with chanting so delightful that no human tongue could ever match it."[98]

Can we even imagine this? What a gift! And it tells us of the rejoicing of angels at such profound times. The professing of vows is a very significant moment in a nun's life when she wholeheartedly gives herself fully to the service of God. And the angels rejoice!

Saint Faustina and the angels

Sister Faustina wrote in her *Diary,* "I thanked God for His goodness, that He gives us angels for companions. Oh, how little people reflect on the fact that they always have beside them such a guest, and at the same time a witness to everything! Remember, sinners, that you likewise have a witness to all your deeds."[99]

In my book *52 Weeks with Saint Faustina: A Year of Grace and Mercy,* I stated:

> Sister Faustina had a very close relationship with her guardian angel and greatly admired St. Michael. As she explained, "I have great reverence for Saint Michael the Archangel; he had no example to follow in doing the will of God, and yet he fulfilled God's will faithfully" (*Diary,* 667). During Adoration one time, Sr. Faustina repeated the prayer "Holy God" several times. "[A] vivid presence of God suddenly swept over me, and I was caught up in spirit before the majesty of God. I saw how the Angels and the Saints of the Lord give glory to God." She couldn't describe it. "The glory of God is so great that I dare not try to describe it, because I would not be able to do so" (*Diary,* 1604). Sister Faustina said she truly understood why St. Paul did not want to describe Heaven (see 1 Cor 2:9 and 2 Cor 12:1-7). In her simplicity, this young nun was absolutely brilliant![100]

How wonderful that Faustina came to know how the angels and saints give glory to God. In addition, what is not to love about her summation of St. Michael's faithful following of God's holy will? Her explanation gives us all a better appreciation for the mighty holy warrior.

One time during Adoration, Sr. Faustina was overcome with love for Jesus. She wrote, "[M]y spirit seemed to be dying for Him." She began to cry. Suddenly, she saw "a spirit of great beauty," who spoke to her, saying, "Don't cry — says the Lord." Faustina asked who he was. He replied, "I am one of the seven spirits who stand before the throne of God day and night and give Him ceaseless praise."

Sister Faustina's experience with this great angel caused her yearning for God to increase. "This spirit is very beautiful," she recalled, "and his beauty comes from close union with God." She was aware of this beautiful spirit in her life and added, "This spirit does not leave me for a single moment, but accompanies me everywhere."[101]

Protection of angels

Throughout Sr. Faustina's amazing journey of Divine Mercy, God saw fit to have angels actively participating to help His "Secretary of Divine Mercy." Since the message of Divine Mercy is very much opposed by the evil one because he doesn't want people to know of God's Mercy, it was necessary to have the protection of holy angels.

You might recall that when our friend was a young girl, Helena would be awakened at night by flashes of light. She believed her Guardian Angel was summoning her to prayer. In addition, as we have discussed, very early in religious life, Sr. Faustina's Guardian Angel escorted her to Purgatory at God's command.

One time on a train journey to Vilnius, Sr. Faustina was very aware of a large radiant angel sitting beside her! No doubt, there might have been other times that an angel or angels were accompanying her, but perhaps not as noticeable to her. Yet, she did note in her *Diary* entry that she had seen this same spirit at

other times, because she said he was, "radiant as at other times."
She also mentions this spirit at other times and had said, "This
spirit does not leave me for a single moment, but accompanies
me everywhere."

She later recalled the train journey in her *Diary*, "Then I
saw one of the seven spirits near me, radiant as at other times,
under a form of light. I constantly saw him beside me when I
was riding on the train. I saw an angel standing on every church
we passed, but surrounded by a light which was paler than that
of the spirit who was accompanying me on the journey, and each
of these spirits who were guarding the churches bowed his head
to the spirit who was near me."[102]

Can we even imagine? I, for one, am very appreciative that
St. Faustina was obedient in writing these experiences in her
Diary. We can greatly benefit from this wisdom.

Sister Faustina's Guardian Angel came to her rescue when
Sr. Faustina needed protection from the devil. The young mystic
recalled, "I fell asleep as soon as I lay down, but at about eleven
o'clock Satan shook my bed. I awoke instantly, and I started to
pray peacefully to my Guardian Angel."[103] This happened after
an incident which occurred in the chapel earlier in the day. I will
share that shortly.

Sister Faustina continued to pray the Rosary because as
she said, "I saw many demons." After many Rosaries, toward
dawn, "these beings vanished." She was finally able to get a bit
of sleep. Jesus consoled His dear Faustina later that morning in
the chapel. We will discuss that in a bit.

Another time, Sr. Faustina was visited by her radiant Guardian Angel and "a flame of fire sparkled from his forehead." Her
Guardian Angel was there to protect her, for a great multitude
of demons, filled with hatred, were blocking the mystic's way.
Sister Faustina immediately beseeched her Guardian Angel for
help. Her angel said, "Do not fear, spouse of my Lord; without
His permission these spirits will do you no harm."

Sister Faustina recounted, "Immediately the evil spirits
vanished, and the faithful Guardian Angel accompanied me, in a
visible manner, right to the very house."[104] Amazing!

Her Guardian Angel called to her

Sister Faustina wrote about her Guardian Angel several times in her *Diary*. For instance, her Guardian Angel at times, instructed her to pray for the dying and other times, came to her rescue (which I mentioned above).

Saint Faustina's Guardian Angel often alerted her about the need for prayers for a dying person. She would then pray fervently for the soul of the dying. As she progressed along the journey of holiness, St. Faustina became more and more aware of the need for prayer and even vividly felt a call from a soul who needed help and was also blessed to have the help of her Guardian Angel.

Saint Faustina wrote, "My Guardian Angel told me to pray for a certain soul, and in the morning I learned that it was a man whose agony had begun that very moment. The Lord Jesus makes it known to me in a special way when someone is in need of prayer. I especially know when my prayer is needed by a dying soul. This happens more often now than it did in the past."[105]

She also wrote, "I feel vividly and clearly that spirit who is asking me for prayer. I was not aware that souls are so closely united, and often it is my Guardian Angel who tells me."[106]

God's wrath, an angel, and reparation

One time, Sr. Faustina experienced quite a scene which involved a mighty angel and the divine wrath of God. Though she might have felt powerless over the circumstances, she called upon the power of Jesus' grace in her soul. I wrote about it in my book *52 Weeks with Saint Faustina*:

> One night in her cell, Sr. Faustina saw a dazzling angel with a glorious face, an 'executor of divine wrath, who appeared on a cloud. "From the cloud, bolts of thunder and flashes of lightning were springing into his hands; and from his hand they were going forth, and only then were they striking the earth." She began to implore the angel to halt when she saw he would strike the earth. She hoped penance could prevent

the punishment. "But my plea was a mere nothing in the face of the divine anger." She then saw the Most Holy Trinity. "The greatness of Its majesty pierced me deeply, and I did not dare to repeat my entreaties. At that very moment, I felt in my soul the power of Jesus' grace, which dwells in my soul. When I became conscious of this grace, I was instantly snatched up before the Throne of God." She said, "Oh, how great is our Lord and God and how incomprehensible His holiness!" She wouldn't attempt to describe the greatness of God. She pleaded with God for the world. "As I was praying in this manner, I saw the Angel's helplessness: he could not carry out the just punishment which was rightly due for sins." She recalled, "Never before had I prayed with such inner power as I did then. The words with which I entreated God are these: Eternal Father, I offer You the Body and Blood, Soul and Divinity of Your dearly beloved Son, Our Lord Jesus Christ for our sins and those of the whole world; for the sake of His sorrowful Passion, have mercy on us" (*Diary*, 474-475). As we know, this prayer makes up part of the Divine Mercy Chaplet.[107]

Holy Communion from an angel!

Many times, because Sr. Faustina suffered from illnesses, she was confined to bed in her cell and not allowed to go to the chapel for Holy Mass or prayers with the other sisters. She accepted this sacrifice as God's holy will for her even though it was difficult because her humble heart yearned to receive her Savior Jesus Christ in Holy Communion.

One time, she was confined to bed because Sr. David said she could not go to the chapel for Holy Communion. Even though, Sr. Faustina felt sad, she calmly resigned herself to God's holy will. She knew that He knew what was best for her and considered Him to be her Divine Physician. Something rather incredible occurred the following day!

A seraph (angel) illuminated by radiant light came to her. He said, "Behold the Lord of Angels," and offered Holy Communion to Sr. Faustina! She was entirely blown away by this mystical and miraculous occurrence. As she expressed, she was, "drowned in the love of God and in amazement."

She later recalled, "The Seraph was surrounded by a great light, the divinity and love of God being reflected in him." She then described him, saying, "He wore a golden robe and, over it, a transparent surplice and a transparent stole. The chalice was crystal, covered with a transparent veil." Sister Faustina wrote in her *Diary*, "As soon as he gave me the Lord, he disappeared."[108] The beautiful seraph visited Sr. Faustina for 13 days, giving her Holy Communion each time!

Jumping ahead for just a moment, I want to mention something interesting. That is, Sister Faustina's spiritual director Fr. Michael Sopoćko visited Faustina (September 26, 1938) shortly before her death. Sister Faustina spoke to him about how her "one occupation is to live in the presence of my Heavenly Father."

Father Sopoćko observed that Sr. Faustina "looked like an unearthly being." He noted in his Memoirs (pg. 5), "At that time, I no longer had the slightest doubt that what she had written in her diary about receiving Holy Communion from an Angel was really true."[109]

Evil prowling about

Just as we said that angels are real, demons are real too. The demons are the rebellious angels. They turned away from God and chose to sin. Though they are invisible, they wage a war against the good. It might seem a bit scary to talk about them, but we should never fear them at all. We should always remember that God is always in control and demons cannot do anything without His permission. Knowing the existence of the devil and demons helps us to be attentive to the spiritual battles in life and to understand why they occur. Basically, it is because the devil desires to drag every single soul to hell. That sounds awful and also very blunt. Yet, it is the evil one's plan in a nut shell.

By living a Christian life, following the Commandments, through prayer and frequenting the Sacraments, the devil's plans can be thwarted to a certain extent. In addition, we can do our very best to be a shining example of God's love to others which will help them on their spiritual journeys so that they may be saved from hell. We can also pray for the conversion of sinners.

Hell and evil might be uncomfortable subjects to discuss. And countless people do not believe in hell's existence. However, it is essential to acknowledge that it does exist and the devil is not some fictitious cartoon character. He takes pleasure in tricking countless souls into sin and ultimately to the eternal punishing flames of hell.

That said, even though it might be uncomfortable to read about such things as evil, I will discuss it here to learn more about St. Faustina's life and also for your own knowledge and preparation in your own spiritual battles.

You might recall that Sr. Faustina was plagued with doubts and confusion at the beginning of religious life. The evil one had his hand in it. However, God allowed these struggles for Faustina's growth in holiness. With time, Sr. Faustina learned to immediately turn over the struggle to God by praying as soon as trouble reared its ugly head.

In spite of the turmoil she often experienced, the young mystic knew that prayer and staying close to Jesus' Heart would be her saving graces. One entry in her *Diary*, revealed her spiritual battles and battle strategies. She wrote, "Despite the peace in my soul, I fight a continuous battle with the enemy of my soul. More and more, I am discovering his traps, and the battle flares up anew." And her approach: "During interludes of calm, I exercise myself and keep watch, lest the enemy find me unprepared. And when I see his great fury, I stay inside the stronghold; that is, the Most Sacred Heart of Jesus."[110]

Faustina's strategy is a wise one we can also strive to put into practice!

Remember, I mentioned earlier, Jesus told Sr. Faustina that the devil absolutely hated her because she snatched so many souls from his dominion. That is because of the great message of Divine Mercy! Jesus wants everyone to know that every single person, even, and most especially, the most hardened sinner is loved by Jesus and can be redeemed by His Love and Mercy. The devil does not want anyone to know this! Plus, he wants to trick people into thinking that hell does not even exist and that there is no consequence for sin. When people believe that, the evil one has got them trapped.

Give up Divine Mercy and prayer for sinners!

The devil had the nerve one evening to try to convince Sr. Faustina to entirely give up on Divine Mercy and not bother praying for sinners. Right before he spoke to her, Sr. Faustina felt a "strange dislike for everything having to do with God" and Satan said, "Think no more about this work. God is not as merciful as you say He is. Do not pray for sinners, because they will be damned all the same, and by this work of mercy you expose your own self to damnation. Talk no more about this mercy of God with your confessor and especially not with Father Sopoćko and Father Andrasz." Sister Faustina noted in her *Diary* that, following these words, "the voice took the appearance of my Guardian Angel."

She said in reply, "I know who you are: the father of lies [cf. Jn 8:44]." Sister Faustina immediately made the Sign of the Cross, and the being vanished, albeit "with a great racket and fury."[111] The devil is not stupid. He was certain of the great importance of the work of Divine Mercy. He attacked Sr. Faustina often, trying to tempt her to doubt God's boundless Mercy. The evil one even knew the names of Sr. Faustina's spiritual directors and disguised himself as her Guardian Angel.

Perhaps ironically, the devil taught something valuable to Sr. Faustina. Through the devil's howling and fury, the young mystic recognized the power and importance in intercessory prayer. The devil tried to threaten Faustina with being damned for praying for sinners. Good thing she was humble and prayerful, or else she could have fallen for it. Would we?

Here's what happened: "Taking the form of an apparition," Sr. Faustina recalled, "he said, 'Do not pray for sinners, but for yourself, for you will be damned.'" So, Faustina paid no attention to Satan. Instead, the young nun prayed hard, redoubling her fervor for sinners. She wrote, "The Evil Spirit howled with fury, 'Oh, if I had power over you!' and disappeared. I saw that my suffering and prayer shackled Satan and snatched many souls from his clutches." So, we learn from Sr. Faustina's experience that the devil does not really have "power over" anyone no matter how scary he appears or howls. We also learn that Sr. Faustina's suffering and prayer "shackled" the devil and stole souls from his clutches! This is good news, indeed! Sister Faustina's prayer efforts stopped Satan in his tracks! We should all strive to redouble our prayer efforts to save souls.[112]

Hell is a reality

Yes, indeed, hell is real. The reality of hell is part of public Revelation. Our loving God, has revealed the reality of hell in the New Testament, and above all in the teachings of Jesus Christ Himself. At times, throughout history, God has reminded us. He has given unique visions and insights to certain souls (saints) for their own sakes, as well as for the benefit of the entire world.

When we pass from this life to the next, we will go to Heaven, hell, or Purgatory. Thankfully, if we go to Purgatory, it will only be for a time of purification (whatever amount of time that might be) and then we will surely go to Heaven when we are ready to see God face-to-face.

The biggest trick of the devil is to convince people that hell is nonexistent and there is no consequence for sin (or breaking God's Commandments). He is the master of lies and seeks to do all the evil he can to destroy us. These are strong words, albeit true. We should not fear because we have God on our side!

One time, an angel led Sr. Faustina to the depths of hell. Faustina described it in great detail in her *Diary*. She expressed, "It is a place of great torture; how awesomely large and extensive it is!" She observed many kinds of torture, which she mentioned in her *Diary*. There's no need to dwell upon each and every torture here. You can read them in her *Diary* (741) if you'd like to learn more.

The important things to remember about hell are that Satan is a liar and doesn't want you to know it exists and there are many tortures awaiting the souls who turn away from God, commit sin, and don't repent of sins.

Saint Faustina was commanded by God to testify to hell's existence and to give a warning. She wrote, "I, Sister Faustina, by the order of God, have visited the abysses of hell so that I might tell souls about it and testify to its existence. I cannot speak about it now; but I have received a command from God to leave it in writing. The devils were full of hatred for me, but they had to obey me at the command of God." And if we think this is bad enough, Sr. Faustina tells us that it is actually worse than she has described. She explained, "What I have written is but a pale shadow of the things I saw." She added a very urgent warning. "But I noticed one thing: that most of the souls there are those who disbelieved that there is a hell." Sister Faustina was so shaken by the experience of being in hell that she "could hardly recover" when she "came to." She couldn't get the suffering of the damned souls off of her mind. She wrote, "How terribly souls suffer there!" This terrifying experience prodded Sr. Faustina to pray even more fervently for souls of sinners to be converted. The humble mystic exclaimed, "I incessantly plead God's mercy upon them. O my Jesus, I would rather be in agony until the end of the world, amidst the greatest sufferings, than to offend You by the least sin."[113]

Now that we know that most of the souls in hell are those who disbelieved in hell in the first place, we should all do our part to educate others about Eternal Life, about making the right choices while there is time while we are here on Earth. We should also try our best to be a good example of a Christian to inspire others to also lead good and holy lives. If the opportunity unfolds to speak the truth about the existence of hell, we shouldn't be afraid to do so. We might be helping to save a soul (or more) from the terrible fate of hell.

I'll mention briefly here that the shepherd children at Fatima: Lucia De Santos, St. Francisco, and St. Jacinta Marto were also shown the vision of hell. The Blessed Mother showed them so that they would know the reality of it and could teach others. In addition, very importantly, that they could pray Rosaries and offer penances for the salvation of souls. Sister Lucia wrote in her *Memoirs* later on that she would have died of fright at the sight of hell if she hadn't already known from the Blessed Mother that she would be going to Heaven. We certainly do not want to go to hell, and should pray that no one else goes there either.

Something to Think About

Take a moment to ponder what you have learned. Heaven and hell are real. Angels and demons are real. Life is a spiritual battle. We fight it all the way to Heaven. Let Heaven always be your goal. Live your life to please Jesus and serve His people. One time, St. Teresa of Calcutta (Mother Terse) told me, "Do everything for the glory of God and the good of His people." Let's strive to do just that.

Take a moment to think about how you can lovingly help someone to realize the need to strive to get to Heaven by leading a holy life. God desires that we care about the souls of sinners just like the Portuguese shepherd children and St. Faustina.

Pray

Dear Jesus and Mary, please guide me to lead a holy life and help others to do so by my prayers, words and example. Jesus, I trust in You! Dear St. Faustina, please pray for me.

A Merciful Action

Strive to be a radiant holy example to others and look for opportunities to teach others about Eternal Life and the need to live holy lives and not get tricked by the devil.

"I see that, in every respect, this work is beyond my strength. I am a little child before the immensity of the task, and it is only at the Lord's clear command that I am setting about to carry it out" (*Diary*, 786).

9

Trust, Trust, and Again Trust!

Sister Faustina always loved God, but she had to learn how to wholeheartedly trust Him with her life. It's something we all have to do. At times, our learning to trust God comes with much difficulty. However, no matter the difficulty, God is teaching us all throughout. We might recall how Helena wanted with all her heart to enter religious life, but her parents wouldn't allow her to.

Stanislaus and Marianna not only refused their daughter once, but at least twice. Most likely, the subject came up again and again. We can imagine Helena's continual disappointment. She also admitted to shunning God's graces because she didn't exactly trust that Almighty God knew what He was doing when He called her to follow Him.

Remember when Helena was knocking on convent doors, hoping to be admitted? Indeed, she needed to trust that Jesus would guide her to the correct convent door, a.k.a. religious congregation, and also later on, in the mission of Divine Mercy. As He promised, Jesus eventually assigned a spiritual director, Fr. Michael Sopoćko (Blessed), to her to help in the mission.

In time, the young nun grew in a deeper understanding of the absolute importance of trusting in God for every single thing. Eventually, she prayed such sentiments as: "Whatever You do with me, Jesus, I will always love You, for I am Yours. Little matter whether You leave me here or put me somewhere else; I am always Yours."[114]

Sister Faustina learned an essential, and sometimes mysterious secret in the spiritual life. That is, Jesus is the Divine Physician, Who knows exactly what we need and when we need it. We might think we know what we need. But that very thing we think is important or that we long for can lead us astray. Jesus, might instead have us undergo a particular trial, sickness, or misunderstanding in order for us to surrender fully to His holy will and earn graces for our own souls and even the souls of others.

Interestingly, as I am writing this chapter for you, my older friend Mary got in touch with me. She had fallen and broken her leg and had to be in a rehab facility throughout part of the Advent season and during Christmas. Mary just informed me that her doctor did not give her the good news she wanted to hear. He said she is not yet ready to go home. Naturally, she was disappointed, but Mary said it took a bit of time, but she has now come to grips with the reality and realizes that in addition to the extra time needed to heal her leg, God is also teaching the virtue of patience to her. She will embrace it and use her time prayerfully and in resignation to God's will for her.

Trust through holy examples

You might remember that when Sr. Faustina was going through a difficult trial, St. Thérèse appeared to her in a dream and told her she needed to trust. She specifically said, "Yes, you will be a saint just as I am, but you must trust in the Lord Jesus."[115] Amazing — a saint was teaching another saint about trust! We can learn from the two of them!

We should consider that our responses to our circumstances have a lot to do with the outcome of our situations. In other words, Faustina would become a canonized saint as St. Thérèse had claimed. However, in order for that to happen, it was necessary for Sr. Faustina to trust God with her life and let Him lead the way. She couldn't become complacent, but rather, she needed to move her will to strive for holiness and accept everything the good Lord gave to her — whether suffering or bliss. He works throughout all of the details of our lives.

Sister Faustina learned a lot about trusting God from the Blessed Mother. As we know, Mary was always involved with the salvation of souls, and the divine work of her Son Jesus. In order for the Blessed Mother to do so, she had to wholeheartedly trust God. Mary suffered intensely, united as she was to her Son. Sister Faustina learned from Mary how to truly love souls — loving them enough to sincerely care about their salvation by bearing sacrifices, all the while, wholeheartedly trusting God.

Many times, (and we see this throughout the *Diary*), the Mother of God spoke to Sr. Faustina about the spiritual life and how she needed to trust God with all her heart. One time, the Blessed Mother explained to Faustina that she should be like a little child before the Lord. Sister Faustina recalled the experience in her *Diary*.

With her familiar fountain pen, she wrote in her *Diary*: "The Blessed Mother was telling me to accept all that God asked of me like a little child, without questioning; otherwise it would not be pleasing to God."[116]

I must make mention here that accepting everything from God does not mean we should accept everything that befalls us in life. In other words, not everything is from God. If there is a wrong (abuse, ill treatment, etc.), it must be corrected. What the Blessed Mother meant was for Sr. Faustina to accept as a child the will of God, even if it was difficult for her to do so because ultimately, God had a perfect plan for her (and for all of us too). That said, God can and will bring good out of the bad things that befall us in life.

Jesus often spoke to Sr. Faustina about trusting Him. Jesus told her, **"The graces of My mercy are drawn by means of one vessel only, and that is — trust. The more a soul trusts, the more it will receive. Souls that trust boundlessly are a great comfort to Me, because I pour all the treasures of My graces into them. I rejoice that they ask for much, because it is My desire to give much, very much. On the other hand, I am sad when souls ask for little, when they narrow their hearts."**[117]

Jesus even taught Faustina that when one wholeheartedly trusts Him, He showers the person with much grace and it overflows out to others. Knowing this should prod us on more heartily to trust God so that the graces not only help us, but those in our midst!

Jesus said, "Tell [all people], **my daughter, that I am Love and Mercy itself. When a soul approaches Me with trust, I fill it with such an abundance of graces that it cannot contain them within itself, but radiates them to other souls."**[118]

Let us trust our Lord with all our hearts!

Trust through ill health and obedience

Come what may, we are to trust God even when the going gets tough, which was often the case with St. Faustina, and with all of the saints, and saints-in-the-making. When we strive to stay on that narrow road that leads to eternal life, we should know that the road will not be a nice and easy straight forward path. There will be bumps in the road! There will be twists and turns and perhaps a few dark corners too. Through it all, we absolutely need to trust God with our lives. We have to stay close to Him and earnestly pray for grace and guidance. He will not abandon us. The journey will be well worth the rewards in Heaven!

Saint Faustina experienced much ill health in her life. It might seem ironic that the once healthy farm girl became sickly after joining religious life. Yet, God allowed her to experience such things in order for her to grow in holiness and in trust of His holy will for her life. Faustina learned the importance of offering everything to Jesus and asking for His holy will to be fulfilled through her life. Her sufferings became redemptive and so very valuable for the salvation of souls.

Even before Sr. Faustina learned the signature line of the Image of the Divine Mercy, "Jesus, I trust in You," Jesus was teaching her about trusting Him. After she was entrusted with the mighty mission of propagating the message of Divine Mercy, she often fell to the floor in earnest prayer, begging our Lord for His help while telling Him that she trusted in Him. The young mystic made many acts of trust and acts of faith. This is something we can do too. Wherever we are, we can make these acts of trust and faith.

Sometimes, trusting God was very confusing to Sr. Faustina. After all, Jesus would tell her one thing and her superiors another.

Who was she to believe? To whom should she obey? Well, even though we might think it should be Jesus, He told His bride Faustina that she should obey her superiors and not Him when they were telling her to do things in contradiction to Him. Jesus told her that He would always be pleased with her obedience to her superiors. Even though, getting anything accomplished in this way might seem impossible, it all always worked out in the end.

Vessels of grace

Jesus bestowed countless blessings and graces upon Sr. Faustina. One time, He told her that she was not always pleased with the vessel of grace. What does this mean? Well, graces come to us in a variety of ways. Remember, I told you (several times!) that Jesus is the Divine Physician and knows exactly what we need and when we need it? Well, He distributes His graces in the most perfect way to help our souls. It's up to us to respond to them with love and gratefulness. I'll give you some examples. First, I'll tell you what Jesus told Faustina.

He said: **"My daughter, do not pay so much attention to the vessel of grace as to the grace itself which I give you, because you are not always pleased with the vessel, and then the graces, too, become deficient. I want to guard you from that, and I want you never to pay attention to the vessel in which I send you My grace. Let all the attention of your soul be concentrated on responding to My grace as faithfully as possible."**[119]

Jesus told Faustina she needed to focus on responding to His grace and not worry about how it comes to her. Consider your own life. Surely, there were times when something seemed out of your control. You prayed. And the seemingly impossible situation ended up resolved even better than you could have imagined.

There might be a time in your life when you experience an uncomfortable sickness or health issue. Of course, you want to get better and it's never wrong to ask God for that. However, during the time of enduring the bit of suffering, you can prayerfully resign yourself to God's will for you. You can even pray that God will grant graces to you and others and you can offer the pain or suffering for the salvation of souls. And because you responded with patience and love, much good can come out of it — for your own soul and even the souls of others.

You might not have chosen a particular "vessel of grace" to come to you. Most of us don't like to deal with such things as a criticism, a loss, a struggle, or some difficulty. However, God knows what is best for our souls. We might not have grown in holiness the same as we would have if we had not experienced the struggle. If we only focus on the struggle, being distracted by it, we might lose out on the graces! That's why Jesus told Faustina not to pay attention to the vessel.

It reminds me of the time I had to be on complete bedrest for almost nine months during a precarious pregnancy. It was difficult for me to stay still for so long (with four children to care for). Plus, there was the grave concern as well. But I needed to follow doctor's orders in order to preserve the life of my unborn baby and for my own health too.

Well, in addition to finally healing up from my heart condition and the large hemorrhage in my uterus by the time my baby was ready to enter the world, truly amazing things occurred that would not have happened in a busy mother's life if I had not been put still. Having to be patient and immobile for the most part for nine months unfolded the opportunity for me to be more attentive to God's whispers to my heart and soul. That is, He had me begin my book career by writing on scraps of paper during my pregnancy! During that pregnancy, I became deeply inspired to write in order to help others get to Heaven!

As I type these words for you, I now realize that my pregnancy with my daughter Mary-Catherine was a huge vessel of grace in so many ways! You see, I have always been deeply grateful for the outcome — a healthy baby — and I also recognized that an unexpected gift coming out of it was also the inspiration to write books, but now, I also see clearly that time of staying still was God's utterly amazing "vessel of grace" for me!

We need to trust God in and through all of the vessels of graces He sends to us!

Potato Miracle!

Speaking of trusting God, our friend Faustina worked hard at trusting and turning to Jesus for every detail in her life and often communicated with Him all along the way. One time, after experiencing a frustrating struggle in the convent's kitchen, the young mystic was rewarded by Jesus with the most unexpected gift.

We already know that Sister Faustina was always eager to please Jesus, her Lord and Master. She was also very obedient to her religious superiors, striving to do every task as best as she could. However, as time went on, and Faustina began to suffer from various illnesses and weaknesses, she struggled to do certain tasks. Sometimes, she was sent away for a short rest to get her health back before returning to her second choir jobs.

I'll tell you what happened one ordinary day when Sr. Faustina needed to trust Jesus with the lifting of heavy steaming hot pots filled with boiling potatoes. You see, during her novitiate, while working with the wards in the kitchen, Sr. Faustina found that she was not strong enough to lift the huge pots of potatoes to drain off the scalding hot water into the kitchen sink. She felt very upset because she was tired of spilling blistering hot water and potatoes all over the floor or half of the potatoes in the sink along with the water. Plus, she didn't want to burn someone or herself in the process!

Sister Faustina decided she needed to speak with the Mother Directress and ask to be excused from that particular task. There were nuns more suitable to handle it. What did the superior say? Well, it was not what Faustina wanted to hear. Sister Faustina detailed it in her *Diary*.

"When I told this to Mother Directress, she said that with time I would get used to it and gain the necessary skill." Faustina knew she wouldn't just "gain the necessary skill." That was not the problem. It was that she was not strong enough to handle the huge pots filled with potatoes. Sister Faustina said she felt she was "growing weaker every day." What could she do? Well, she recalled it in her *Diary*. She wrote:

So I would move away when it was time to drain the potatoes. The sisters noticed that I avoided this task and were very much surprised. They did not know that I could not help in spite of all my willingness to do this and not spare myself. At noon, during the examination of conscience, I complained to God about my weakness. Then I heard the following words in my soul, **From today on you will do this easily; I shall strengthen you.**[120]

Can we imagine this? Jesus' words alone must have strengthened Sr. Faustina. Indeed, the young nun felt a renewed strength. I'll let her tell you what happened.

That evening, when the time came to drain off the water from the potatoes, I hurried to be the first to do it, trusting in the Lord's words. I took up the pot with ease and poured off the water perfectly. But when I took off the cover to let the potatoes steam off, I saw there in the pot, in the place of the potatoes, whole bunches of red roses, beautiful beyond description. I had never seen such roses before. Greatly astonished and unable to understand the meaning of this, I heard a voice within me saying, **I change such hard work of yours into bouquets of most beautiful flowers, and their perfume rises up to My throne.** From then on I have tried to drain the potatoes myself, not only during my week when it was my turn to cook, but also in replacement of other sisters when it was their turn. And not only do I do this, but I try to be the first to help in any other burdensome task, because I have experienced how much this pleases God.[121]

If Jesus' words of promise were not enough — imagine this — a miracle too! Jesus performed a great and beautiful miracle for His little Faustina.

Sister Faustina desired to tell us something more. She punctuated this entry in her *Diary* with these words, "O inexhaustible treasure of purity of intention which makes all our actions perfect and so pleasing to God!"[122]

We can consider our own work, play, study, relationships, and vocation. Do we trust Jesus with every little thing in our lives? If not, why not? Sister Faustina's experience and summation of it give a wonderful example to us. "Purity of intention" "makes all our actions perfect and so pleasing to God!" Let's think about that!

The famous *Diary*

The *Diary,* so well-known all around the world, is often associated with St. Faustina and vice versa. Saint Faustina's *Diary* is truly a remarkable treasure trove. We need to deeply explore it here, for it is a deep source of spiritual nourishment, as well as a reference and authority of rich history.

Let's dig in!

How did the *Diary* come about? Was it that Sr. Faustina decided on her own to write it? Was she trying to draw attention to herself? I have mentioned the *Diary* and have referred to it often thus far in this book. Now, we shall finally delve into the origin and meaning of the *Diary,* as well as why it is such a help to us in our own spiritual lives.

Sister Faustina explained her task and difficulty of writing the *Diary* and etched these words on her pages:

> I am to write down the encounters of my soul with You, O God, at the moments of Your special visitations. I am to write about You, O Incomprehensible in mercy towards my poor soul. Your holy will is the life of my soul. I have received this order through him who is for me Your representative here on earth, who interprets Your holy Will to me. Jesus, You see how difficult it is for me to write, how unable I am to put down clearly what I experience in my soul. O God, can a pen write down that for which many a time there are no words? But You give me the order to write, O God; that is enough for me.[123]

With regard to Faustina writing the *Diary,* Jesus explained to her, "**Secretary of My most profound mystery, know that yours is an exclusive intimacy with Me. Your task is to write down everything that I make known to you about My mercy, for the benefit of those who by reading these things will be comforted in their souls and will have the courage to approach Me**."[124]

It was within the last four years of St. Faustina's life when the young mystic actively wrote the six notebooks that were later referred to as: "the Diary of St. Faustina" or titled, "*Diary of Saint Maria Faustina Kowalska: Divine Mercy in My Soul*." This compilation of once handwritten notebooks later became one of the most popular books in the world! In her beautiful penmanship, Sr. Faustina wrote her first writings on loose sheets of paper. Afterwards, she wrote in six bound notebooks, filled out on both sides of the pages. Father Sopoćko asked Sr. Faustina to underline Jesus' words in pencil and he read her writings at the convent.

She wrote in secret

When Sr. Faustina (Helena at the time) entered religious life, probably the farthest thing from her mind was that she would be writing a bunch of notebooks in secret. And these were not just ordinary notebooks! They contained experiences with and revelations from Jesus Christ Himself! In addition, they contained the Mother of God's communications to Faustina, as well as many teachings and experiences with her other contacts from the supernatural world, such as: angels, saints, Holy Souls in Purgatory, and attacks by the devil. It was no easy task for her to write about herself or any of the above.

Why did Sr. Faustina write in secret? It was simply because she did not want anyone seeing what she wrote. And why did she write in the first place? Well, Jesus told her to! He said, "**[W]rite down these words… Tell the world about my Mercy and my love. The flames of Mercy are burning me. I desire to pour them out upon human souls. Oh, what pain they cause Me when they do not want to accept them! My daughter,**

do whatever is within your power to spread devotion to My Mercy. I will make up for what you lack."[125]

As we know, St. Faustina experienced many trials and tribulations trying to get religious superiors to believe her experiences with Jesus. Finally, as we know already, she was given a spiritual Director, Father Michael Sopoćko. He instructed her to write down everything in a *Diary*. You see, Fr. Sopoćko told Sr. Faustina to write down her experiences so that he could read them thoroughly and be better able to discern what was going on in her life than he would through just hearing her tell him while in the confessional. Besides, Sr. Faustina was taking an awfully long time in the confessional attempting to tell her director what Jesus was revealing to her heart. This caused prolonged time for Fr. Sopoćko too, and possibly other sisters getting annoyed. The superiors gave their consent to Fr. Sopoćko's orders.

So, Faustina trusted Jesus and her director and she wrote and she wrote, and she wrote! She never once thought she had a talent for writing and she had to fit all of this writing in between her duties and prayer times. At times, she had to quickly hide her writing — as when someone unexpectedly showed up at her cell. There were other obstacles as well.

I think you might smile when you read dear Faustina's heartfelt words to Jesus about her difficulty in writing the *Diary*. She even complained to Jesus about her pen!

She said, "My Jesus, You see that I do not know how to write well and, on top of that, I don't even have a good pen." It's actually heartwarming to "hear" her speak to Jesus in this way. She then told Him, "And often it scratches so badly that I must put sentences together, letter by letter."

But she has more to tell Jesus! "And that is not all." She said. "I also have the difficulty of keeping secret from the sisters the things I write down, and so I often have to shut my notebook every few minutes and listen patiently to someone's story, and then the time set aside for writing is gone."

Another problem arose for the obedient writer. "And when I shut the notebook suddenly, the ink smears. I write with the permission of my superiors and at the command of my confessor.

It is a strange thing: sometimes the writing goes quite well, but at other times, I can hardly read it myself."[126]

I hope you smiled. Our friend Faustina is very endearing. Yet, writing the *Diary* was no funny business, nor was it for the faint of heart. Sister Faustina wholeheartedly obeyed Jesus and her spiritual director to put very important words down on paper that you and I can read all these years later. The words from the *Diary* are profound truths in the spiritual life — words that can greatly aid us all on our journeys. In the *Diary*, we have been gifted a treasure trove and are essentially allowed in to the journey of a young mystic's soul.

Problems with the *Diary*

Still, another problem unfolded with the *Diary*. But this one is a huge one! Sister Faustina actually burned her *Diary*! I'm sure you might wonder why she would do such a thing. After all, she was so obedient in writing the *Diary* in the first place. The answer is simply that the devil tricked her into doing so. It was when Fr. Sopoćko went away to the Holy Land for a few weeks in 1934. The devil appeared to her as an angel and caused her to doubt herself, filling her head with thoughts that she was only writing the *Diary* because she was prideful.

Because of this, there is no chronological order to the *Diary*. Father Sopoćko directed Sr. Faustina to rewrite the *Diary* anew as a penance. She began this task in July 1934, painstakingly keeping everything extremely accurate. Father explains, "I directed her to rewrite the destroyed contents as a penance. At the same time, she was having new experiences, which she also noted down, interweaving them with what she recalled from the burned notebook. This is why there is no chronological order in her notebooks."[127]

Sister Faustina's writings continued to flow from her pen in Vilnius and Kraków from 1934 to 1938 as she expressed God's unfathomable merciful love for His children and recalled her many mystical experiences. Father Sopoćko continued to read Faustina's writings while becoming very united to the message. It was crystal clear — God personally chose him to spiritually direct the Secretary of Divine Mercy. Being a well-trained theologian, Fr. Sopoćko acted very prudently because he discovered early on that some of what Sr. Faustina wrote seemed a bit unorthodox. Eventually, he saw it was all authentic. He told Sr. Faustina:

> If the things you are telling me really come from God, prepare your soul for great suffering. You will encounter disapproval and persecution. They will look upon you as a hysteric and an eccentric, but the Lord will lavish His graces upon you. True works of God always meet opposition and are marked by suffering. If God wants to accomplish something, sooner or later He will do so in spite of the difficulties. Your part, in the meantime, is to arm yourself with great patience.[128]

Desiring to help others get to Heaven, our Sister Faustina poured herself out until the very end. She wrote the last of her *Diary* in June 1938, just a few months before her death. She expressed, "Although I am feeling weak, and my nature is clamoring for rest," nevertheless she said, "I feel the inspiration of grace telling me to take hold of myself and write, write for the comfort of souls, whom I love so much and with whom I will share all eternity. And I desire eternal life for them so ardently that that is why I use all my free moments, no matter how short, for writing in the way that Jesus wishes of me."[129]

A few pages in the *Diary* were left empty. Experts believe that Sr. Faustina left the pages blank in order to come back to them later. The original manuscript is in excellent shape; yet, one page is missing and is noted as missing in the finished publication. No one knows who tore the page from the notebook. Could it have been Faustina?

One final problem

One final, yet enormous problem developed with regard to the *Diary*. That is, it was not believed! It is because of a poor translation from the Polish, which not only prolonged the Church's final approval, but at one point it deemed the *Diary* as heretical! This certainly seems like the evil one had his hand in all of this.

After all, he does not want the world to know of God's unfathomable Love and Mercy. However, God always wins!

You see, after her death, St. Faustina's writings remained in the Congregation's custody. Eventually, the notebooks were transcribed and typed up. However, this process was done with numerous errors and Jesus' words were not underlined as was the initial instruction. Therefore, the messages were confusing and in 1959, the Holy See banned the spreading of the Divine Mercy message and devotion in the forms conveyed by Sr. Faustina.

As I noted in *52 Weeks with Saint Faustina*:

> Fortunately, the manuscript was transcribed a second time for the Informative Process, part of the investigation needed for Sr. Faustina's beatification. This was done from the original. It was carefully collated by Fr. Isidore Borkiewicz, OFM Conv, and Sr. Beata Piekut, OLM. The translation and typescript were certified by the Metropolitan Curia in Krakow on October 19, 1967. The photocopies of the original manuscript were also sent to Rome. Vice-Promoter of the Faith Fr. George Mrówczynski and Sr. Beata Piekut, OLM, prepared this copy of the *Diary*, along with footnotes and indices, all of which was sent to Fr. Anthony Mruk, SJ, the general postulator (or the person in charge of pursuing the canonization of a particular person) working on the beatification process in Rome. The work was later published in Polish in Rome for the first time in 1981, and then in Poland. This accurate edition has been the source text for any further translations.[130]

"Enlightened interpreter" of Divine Mercy

With regard to the beauty of St. Faustina's obedience and her words etched upon the pages of the *Diary*, Saint John Paul II conveyed St. Faustina's beloved relationship with Jesus and her responsibility in conveying the message of Divine Mercy in the *Diary*.

He wrote: "[Saint Faustina] was chosen by Christ to be a particularly enlightened interpreter of the truth of Divine Mercy. For Sister Faustina, this truth led to an extraordinarily rich mystical life. She was a simple, uneducated person, and yet those who read the *Diary* of her revelations are astounded by the depth of her mystical experience."[131]

Father Sopoćko had no idea that his "student's" *Diary* would later be considered a gem of mystical literature. Some say, after the Bible, the *Diary* is one of the most widely read religious works in the world! An article in *L'Osservatore Romano* pointed out that "[St.] Faustina's work sheds light on the mystery of the Divine Mercy. It delights not only simple, uneducated people, but also scholars, who look upon it as an additional source of theological research."[132]

Saint John Paul II expressed, "To those who survived the Second World War, Saint Faustina's *Diary* appears as a particular Gospel of Divine Mercy, written from a twentieth-century perspective."[133]

The *Diary,* now translated into twenty languages is cherished by Catholics around the world. It is recognized in the Roman Breviary as "among the outstanding works of mystical literature."

Jesus told Faustina, **"You will prepare the world for My final coming."**[134] In Faustina's obedience to Jesus and her director, that is precisely what she was doing. Her words in the *Diary* prepare us for Jesus' Final coming! Thank God for St. Faustina's great trust in Him and her obedience to write the *Diary*, which we can all benefit from now!

Embracing the Cross of Jesus

While we are in a chapter all about trusting God, we need to discuss the Cross of Jesus. There are times in our lives when we can easily trust God. But how difficult it is for us to trust God when we are heavily burdened. Jesus on the Cross trusted His Father in Heaven. He suffered immensely even though He was the Son of God. We will suffer in this life — it is inevitable. However, we can offer our sufferings to Jesus and ask Him to unite them to His Passion and to redeem us and others. Jesus will grant us graces for the asking.

We must trust Him. We must do as St. Faustina did when she doubted. She made many "Acts of Trust." She often fell to the floor under the weight of the heavy burden afflicting her. And sometimes, with arms outstretched in the form of a cross, Faustina cried out to Jesus for help. At times, her cries were earnestly simple, but coming from the depths of her heart. She told Jesus that she trusted Him no matter what was going on.

The Blessed Mother impressed upon St. Faustina that in faithfully following God's holy will, she would encounter His Holy Cross. Being a Catholic or Christian is all about being connected with the Cross of Christ.

In other words, if everything we desired was given to us like spoiled children, we might not make it to Heaven. That is because our pilgrimage here on Earth is not supposed to be all about being comfortable and pleasing ourselves at all costs. In order to get to Heaven, we must follow God's holy will in our lives. Again, we are reminded of Jesus' teaching to deny ourselves, pick up our cross and follow Him.

Saint Faustina learned much from Jesus' Cross and redemptive suffering in carrying out the mission of Divine Mercy entrusted to her. By "redemptive" we mean that God can bring much good out of our sufferings when we lovingly offer them to Him. We can become bitter or angry, we can try to run away, or we can resign ourselves to the fact that God knows what He is doing and He gives us what we need. Again and again, we need to trust Him as a Divine Physician.

Saint Faustina's life seemed to be a mix of great grace and intense suffering. She received much grace in the mission of Divine Mercy, but at times, even the graces seemed too much for her to bear and the weight of the mission bore down on her — sometimes to the point of collapsing. I'll let the young mystic herself explain this:

> During Vespers today, an unusual pain pierced my
> soul. I see that, in every respect, this work is beyond
> my strength. I am a little child before the immensity

of the task, and it is only at the Lord's clear command that I am setting about to carry it out. On the other hand, even these great graces are a burden for me, and I am barely able to carry them. I see my superiors' disbelief and doubts of all kinds and, for this reason, their apprehensive behavior towards me. My Jesus, I see that even such great graces can be [a source of] suffering. And yet, it is so; not only may they be a cause of suffering, but they must be such, as a sign of God's action. I understand well that if God himself did not strengthen the soul in these various ordeals, the soul would not be able to master the situation. Thus God himself is its shield.[135]

We can certainly learn much from St. Faustina's words above. Yes, it was difficult, however, God had a plan. He always does. It often includes the pin pricks and sufferings required for a soul to respond lovingly to God and embrace the Cross in order for many fruits to burst forth.

The Blessed Virgin Mary shared an important truth with St. Faustina. She told her daughter Faustina that even though she was the Mother of God, she did not escape suffering. We might be amazed at this. Specifically she said, "*Know, My daughter, that although I was raised to the dignity of Mother of God, seven swords of pain pierced My heart. Don't do anything to defend yourself; bear everything with humility; God Himself will defend you.*"[136] Imagine hearing from the Mother of God about her suffering and that God Himself will defend you!

Will pigs fly?

There are times in life when we might need to speak up to right a wrong. We can pray about what to do and also seek wisdom from someone who can help us.

In Sr. Faustina's case, she was very pleasing in God's eyes when she bore wrongs quietly without defending herself as the Mother of God had instructed. Quite often, Sr. Faustina was the brunt of one sister or another's bad jokes or insults. She was accused of being a hysteric who wanted to be coddled. Though this sarcasm and mean spiritedness is always uncalled for, Sr. Faustina advanced in holiness through her act of not defending herself, but rather returning a kind word, and always a prayer for the person.

In fact, Jesus taught Faustina to not only love her enemies and those who did ill to her (as the Bible tells us to do), but to also do good to them (see Matthew 5:43-48). One way to do this is to pray for the person who has done wrong.

Speaking of insults aimed at Faustina, one time, Sr. Chrysostom Korczak, a sister working in the infirmary with Sr. Faustina overheard the murmurings about Sr. Faustina's mystical experiences and did not believe them. In fact, the rumors made her very upset! Snarling in anger, Sr. Chrysostom sarcastically asked, "Sister, you want to be a saint?" But before Sr. Faustina could respond, Sr. Chrysostom fired away, "Pigs will fly before that'll happen."

We might laugh because the skeptical sister actually said such things to the very virtuous St. Faustina. We should hope the sister acted with virtue as well. After all, she was also called to be a saint-in-the-making, striving for holiness in religious life. But let's see what Sr. Faustina said in return.

"Sister, I love you even more."[137]

Eyes fixed on the Cross

The Blessed Mother instructed St. Faustina one time to do what she herself had done — to keep her eyes fixed on the Cross even in times of joy. In other words, not to forget Jesus' great Love and Mercy for her and for all of His children and what He had to go through to open the gates of Heaven for us. Saint Faustina noted in her *Diary*, "[A]nd She told me that the graces God was granting me were not for me alone, but for other souls as well."[138]

Speaking of keeping our eyes on the Cross of Jesus, one time, Jesus told Sr. Faustina, **"There is more merit to one hour of meditation on My sorrowful Passion than there is to a whole year of flagellation that draws blood; the contemplation of My painful wounds is of great profit to you, and it brings Me great joy."**[139]

Faustina recalled in her *Diary*, "Jesus told me that I please Him best by meditating on His sorrowful Passion, and by such meditation much light falls upon my soul."[140]

Jesus also told her, **"There are few souls who contemplate My Passion with true feeling; I give great graces to souls who meditate devoutly on My Passion."**[141] Indeed, this is something for us to ponder.

In my own life, I was blessed to know St. Teresa of Calcutta for about ten years. Because of a lot of suffering in my life, Mother Teresa told me that I had come so close to Jesus on the Cross that He could kiss me!

She also said, "In all of our lives suffering has to come. Suffering is the kiss of Jesus, a sign that you have come so close to Jesus on the Cross that He can kiss you."[142] And she then asked me to offer some of my sufferings for the poor she served. Mother Teresa also shared with me in another letter:

> Jesus shares His love with you and shares His suffering and pain. He is a God of love and does not want His children to suffer, but when you accept your pain, suffering, death and resurrection your pain becomes redemptive for yourself and for others. ... Let us allow Jesus to use us without consulting us by taking what He gives and giving what He takes.[143]

Mother Teresa was emphasizing the fact that our Lord Jesus is the Divine Physician, Who knows exactly what we need and when we need it. Sometimes, Jesus allows us to undergo a trial or tribulation by taking something away from us and at other times, by giving us something to endure.

We should never fear any suffering we are called to endure. We need to remember that God knows exactly what He is doing and will never abandon us — we have to trust Him. Eventually, with God's grace, we will learn to embrace the Cross, knowing that it is what is best for us because it is precisely what God chooses for us. Embracing the cross always leads to victory and a more perfect union with our Lord and Savior Jesus Christ!

Jesus, Mary, and our saintly friends St. Faustina, St. Thérèse, Mother Teresa, and other saints teach us how to trust God with our lives. Let's allow the nourishment from this chapter to sink into our hearts and souls.

 ## Something to Think About

Take a few moments to ponder what you have learned about St. Faustina and the spiritual life in this chapter. Consider that it takes time to learn to wholeheartedly trust God with our lives. However, we can certainly learn from the examples of St. Faustina and other saints, who have striven for holiness.

Let us remember Faustina's words and strive to also speak to our Lord in this way, trusting that He knows what is best. "Whatever You do with me, Jesus, I will always love You, for I am Yours. Little matter whether You leave me here or put me somewhere else; I am always Yours."

Also, remember the Blessed Mother asked Faustina to behave as a little child before God and accept whatever it is He sent to her.

Do you remember what our friend Faustina said after the beautiful and amazing potato miracle? Remember, she trusted Jesus for the strength to do the task of lifting the huge heavy pots? Well, after that experience, she noted in her *Diary*, "I try to be the first to help in any other burdensome task, because I have experienced how much this pleases God."[144]

Can you strive to do well the burdensome tasks to please God?

Can you pray for the graces to be more trusting of God's holy will for your life?

In addition, can you consider how Jesus told our friend Faustina to handle difficult people and situations?

Remember? Think about all these things.

Pray

Dear Jesus and Mary, please guide me. Help me to sincerely love all people and to strive to carry my personal cross lovingly. Jesus, I trust in You! Dear St. Faustina, please pray for me.

A Merciful Action

Pray to be more trusting of God and endeavor to soon help someone who is struggling in life and has trouble believing in and trusting God.

Jesus said,
"I am giving you three ways of exercising mercy toward your neighbor: the first — by deed, the second — by word, the third — by prayer. In these three degrees is contained the fullness of mercy, and it is an unquestionable proof of love for Me. By this means a soul glorifies and pays reverence to My mercy (*Diary*, 742)."

10

Divine Mercy for Our Souls

Saint Faustina wrote, "God's love is the flower — Mercy the fruit."[145] In this chapter, we will discuss our own personal call to holiness and how Divine Mercy touches our souls and the souls of others.

Our friend St. Faustina told Jesus, "My Jesus, You know that from my earliest years I have wanted to become a great saint; that is to say, I have wanted to love You with a love so great that there would be no soul who has hitherto loved You so. At first these desires of mine were kept secret, and only Jesus knew of them. But today I cannot contain them within my heart; I would like to cry out to the whole world, 'Love God, because He is good and great is His mercy!'"[146]

Saint Faustina's words can deeply stir our own hearts. Let us heed dear St. Faustina's advice! We learn the need to turn to God's mercy and to also offer God's mercy to others from the humble mystic. We can turn to God's mercy on a regular basis in striving for holiness. And sometimes in life, we are brought to our knees in seeking God's mercy due to strenuous circumstances beyond our control. In either case, we most certainly need God's mercy.

In this chapter, we will talk about the need for humility in life, the frequent use of the Church's Sacraments for strength in the spiritual battle throughout life, as well as lessons from Jesus in the spiritual life, wisdom gleaned from the "school of St. Faustina," necessary "degrees of mercy," and so much more. Feel free to take your time with this chapter.

Humility is essential

Sister Faustina was constantly reminded by Jesus, Mary, and the holy ones in her life to remain humble. After all, she was given a very holy mission and it was important that she did not let it get to her head! One time Jesus told Sr. Faustina, **"Although My greatness is beyond understanding, I commune only with those who are little. I demand of you a childlike spirit.**"[147]

Sister Faustina once wrote, "O my God, I understand well that You demand this spiritual childhood of me, because You are constantly asking it of me through Your representatives."[148]

The young nun continually opened her mind, heart, and soul to learn more about herself in light of the holy mission entrusted to her. She reflected upon it often and recorded in her *Diary* how Jesus opened her eyes about what she called her "abyss of misery," and that she understood that all good in her came exclusively from God. While Sr. Faustina's description of herself as an "abyss of misery" might sound a bit extreme to us, let's allow her to explain.

Faustina wrote:

At the beginning of my religious life, suffering and adversities frightened and disheartened me. So I prayed continuously, asking Jesus to strengthen me and to grant me the power of His Holy Spirit that I might carry out His holy will in all things, because from the beginning I have been aware of my weakness. I know very well what I am of myself, because for this purpose Jesus has opened the eyes of my soul; I am an abyss of misery, and hence I understand that whatever good there is in my soul consists solely of His holy grace. The knowledge of my own misery allows me, at the same time, to know the immensity of Your mercy. In my own interior life, I am looking with one eye at the abyss of my misery and baseness, and with the other, at the abyss of Your mercy, O God.[149]

Let us remember, Jesus taught in the Beatitudes: "Blessed

are the poor in spirit, for theirs is the kingdom of heaven." (Mt 5:3) Sister Faustina wrote in her *Diary*, "Today, as God's Majesty swept over me, my soul understood that the Lord, so very great though He is, delights in humble souls."[150]

Certainly, our Lord is delighted with humble souls. Saint Faustina explained in her *Diary*: "The more a soul humbles itself, the greater the kindness with which the Lord approaches it. Uniting himself closely with it, He raises it to His very throne. Happy is the soul whom the Lord himself defends. I have come to know that only love is of any value; love is greatness; nothing, no works, can compare with a single act of pure love of God."[151]

Without humility we are not pleasing to God

Saint Faustina's spiritual director Fr. Sopoćko told Faustina, "Without humility, we cannot be pleasing to God."[152] Sister Faustina came to realize the holy mystery in learning true humility. She wrote, "He who wants to learn true humility should reflect upon the Passion of Jesus. When I meditate upon the Passion of Jesus, I get a clear understanding of many things I could not comprehend before." Our friend Faustina understood that she should strive to imitate and even resemble Jesus. She continued in her *Diary*, "I want to resemble You, O Jesus, — You crucified, tortured, and humiliated. Jesus, imprint upon my heart and soul Your own humility. I love You Jesus ... ."[153]

The Blessed Mother also impressed upon Faustina the importance of the virtue of humility. On December 8, 1937 on the Feast of the Immaculate Conception of the Blessed Virgin Mary, the Blessed Mother made herself known to Sr. Faustina. As we mentioned earlier, the Mother of God smiled at the young nun, told her that she was in an exclusive way, Sr. Faustina's Mother and desired that Faustina consider her a Mother as well.

But in addition to these beautiful words from the Blessed Mother, Mary told Sr. Faustina about the three virtues closest to her, which became engraved upon the young mystic's heart. Specifically, Mary enlightened her with these words:

I desire, My dearly beloved daughter, that you practice the three virtues that are dearest to Me — and most pleasing to God. The first is humility, humility, and once again humility; the second virtue, purity; the third virtue, love of God. As My daughter, you must especially radiate with these virtues." When the conversation ended, She pressed me to Her Heart and disappeared. When I regained the use of my senses, my heart became so wonderfully attracted to these virtues; and I practice them faithfully. They are as though engraved in my heart.[154]

We see how important the virtue of humility is to Jesus and Mary!

The young mystic certainly learned much in the spiritual life and passed it down to all of us. She lets us in on her discovery of meditating upon Jesus's Passion. Jesus Himself, many times instructed His saint-in-the-making to lovingly meditate upon His sufferings and advance in holiness.

In my book, *52 Weeks with Saint Faustina: A Year of Grace and Mercy,* I wrote:

Humility is a precious virtue in the spiritual life. The devil absolutely hates humility. He flees from it. He can't get his way with a humble soul. Saint Vincent de Paul said, "The most powerful weapon to conquer the devil is humility. For, as he does not know at all how to employ it, neither does he know how to defend himself from it.[155]

It is indeed essential for all of us to pray for the virtue of humility so that God will dwell within us and use us to help others. Sister Faustina teaches us to recognize that all good in us comes from God, that we should be grateful for God's providence, and to remain humble, living a spiritual childhood. Because Sr. Faustina was humbly docile to the Holy Spirit, God used her for the great mission of telling the world about His great Love and Mercy, specifically through the Image of the Divine Mercy which Jesus showed to Sr. Faustina on February 22, 1931. God also communicated His Love through the Feast of Mercy and prayers of Divine Mercy, specifically the Chaplet of Divine Mercy and the Novena of Divine Mercy. Jesus desires that the world know about His Mercy now while He is a Merciful Judge and not later as a Just Judge.

The school of St. Faustina

Saint Faustina learned much about the virtues and particularly the virtue of humility. She wrote in her *Diary* a teaching and explanation of humility which she addressed to Jesus telling how God works in a humble soul. We might be tempted to flee from humiliations, but the humble mystic's words are wonderful spiritual guidance for us all.

She wrote:

O my Jesus, nothing is better for the soul than humiliations. In contempt is the secret of happiness, when the soul recognizes that, of itself, it is only wretchedness and nothingness, and that whatever it possesses of good is a gift of God. When the soul sees that everything is given it freely and that the only thing it has of itself is its own misery, this is what sustains it in a continual act of humble prostration before the majesty of God. And God, seeing the soul in such a disposition, pursues it with His graces. As the soul continues to immerse itself more deeply into the abyss of its nothingness and need, God uses His omnipotence to exalt it. If there is a truly happy soul upon earth, it can only be a truly humble soul. At first, one's self-love suffers greatly on this account, but after a soul has struggled courageously, God grants it much light by which it sees how wretched and full of deception everything is. God alone is in its heart. A humble soul does not trust itself, but places all its confidence in God. God defends the humble soul and lets Himself into its secrets, and the soul abides in unsurpassable happiness which no one can comprehend.[156]

Quite often, when Sr. Faustina took a retreat, she benefited from the instruction of Jesus Himself! One time, as the young nun was finishing up a retreat, she gave thanks to Jesus for His "inconceivable kindness," calling Him her "Eternal Love." Jesus responded to her loving praise with additional instruction. He told her:

My daughter, let three virtues adorn you in a particular way: humility, purity of intention and love. Do nothing beyond what I demand of you, and accept everything that My hand gives you. Strive for a life of recollection so that you can hear My voice, which is so soft that only recollected souls can hear it...[157]

Saint Faustina performed little sacrifices whenever she could to earn grace for herself and others. On April 25, 1933, St. Faustina wrote in her *Diary* about "Small Mortifications." She listed:

To recite the Chaplet of The Divine Mercy with outstretched arms.
On Saturday, to say five decades of the Rosary with outstretched arms.
To sometimes recite a prayer [while] lying prostrate.
On Thursdays, a Holy Hour.
On Fridays, some greater mortification for dying sinners.[158]

We too, can strive to do little or big mortifications in order to earn grace and save souls. We can all ponder the divine wisdom of Jesus and also Sr. Faustina's words to Jesus about the virtue of humility and strive to apply it to our own lives.

Sacraments

It is impossible to get to Heaven if we Catholics are not nourished with the Sacraments. Indeed, we need the Sacraments for spiritual survival. But what is a Sacrament? The *Catechism of the Catholic Church* instructs: "The sacraments are efficacious signs of grace, instituted by Christ and entrusted to the Church, by which divine life is dispensed to us. The visible rites by which the sacraments are celebrated signify and make present the graces proper to each sacrament. They bear fruit in those who receive them with the required dispositions."(1131)

By this, we mean, a Sacrament is a sacred and visible sign instituted by Jesus to give us the undeserved gift of grace. It's important to know that Jesus Christ is present at every Sacrament celebrated, just as He was when He established the Sacraments more than 2,000 years ago. The *Catechism* teaches that the seven Sacraments touch all the stages of Christian life (1210). These are: Baptism, Reconciliation, Eucharist, Confirmation, Anointing of the Sick, Holy Orders and Matrimony.

We will focus on two Sacraments that are important for us to frequent in the spiritual life. They are: Confession and the Eucharist.

Confession is powerful!

One time St. Faustina went to confession after not going for a few weeks due to illness. She was eager to confess to Father Andrasz and proceeded to do so as soon as he entered her cell. During which time, she felt a great deal of peace. She also "felt unusually happy to be able to say everything as [she] did." Afterwards, as she recalled in her *Diary*, "Suddenly his figure became diffused with a great light, and I saw that it was not Father A., but Jesus. His garments were bright as snow, and He disappeared immediately." Sister Faustina reflected upon "the fact that Jesus heard the confession in the same way that confessors do."[159]

We should remember that when we go to Confession, we are actually confessing our sins to Jesus Himself, for Whom the priests stands in. Jesus said, **"I Myself am waiting there for you. I am only hidden by the priest ... I, Myself, act in your soul."**[160]

With regard to going to Confession, Jesus said, "**[I]n the Tribunal of Mercy** [the Sacrament of Reconciliation] **There the greatest miracles take place** [and] **are incessantly repeated.**"[161] Jesus further revealed to His Secretary of Divine Mercy, "**[When] you go to confession, to this fountain of My mercy, the Blood and Water which came forth from My heart always flows down upon your soul and enables it.**" Jesus told Faustina to entirely and with great trust immerse herself in His mercy each time she went to Confession so that He may "pour the bounty" of His "grace upon" her "soul." Jesus explained that in the confessional, "**Here the misery of the soul meets the God of mercy.**"

Importantly, we should take to our hearts what Jesus next told His daughter Faustina. "**Tell souls that from this fount of mercy souls draw graces solely with the vessel of trust. If their trust is great, there is no limit to My generosity. The torrents of grace inundate humble souls. The proud remain always in poverty and misery, because My grace turns away from them to humble souls.**"[162] We might recall now the lessons on humility we learned above, as well as the importance of trusting Jesus.

Exorcists have stated that the Sacrament of Confession is a thousand times more powerful than an exorcism. Monsignor Stephen J. Rossetti, Ph.D., exorcist and author said, "The most powerful thing that the Church offers to cast out demons is the confessional. Plus Mass, of course, and the Eucharist. So, go to confession."[163] We need to humble ourselves and frequent the confessional. We can then experience great peace in our hearts.

My friend Fr. Andrew Apostoli, CFR, of happy memory, recommended that I go to Confession every month. Fatima expert that he was, he suggested to go to the Sacrament of Reconciliation on every First Saturday, (which is part of the First Saturday devotion given to us by Our Lady of Fatima). Of course, you can go more often if you'd like, but at least once a month is a good rule of thumb in this regard.

Within this Sacrament, the humble souls receive much grace to resist future temptation. So, Confession not only frees the penitent of sin, cleansing their soul, but it also provides grace to do a better job in the future in resisting the temptation to sin.

Holy Communion

The Church teaches that the Eucharist is the "source and summit" of the Christian life. (*CCC*, 1324-1327) Saint John Paul II stated, "The Eucharist, as Christ's saving presence in the community of the faithful and its spiritual food, is the most precious possession which the Church can have in her journey through history."[164]

Holy Communion, or the Eucharist is such an important Sacrament. After all, it is the gift of Jesus Himself! It is the miracle of Jesus coming to us through bread and wine which has been transubstantiated at the consecration by the priest at holy Mass. I know these are big words, indeed! It basically means that because of God's loving miracle and through the action of the priest, we are given the gift of Jesus: Body Blood, Soul, and Divinity in Holy Communion! Specifically, at the words of Jesus Christ spoken through the priest and the invocation of the Holy Spirit, the bread and wine become the Body and Blood of Christ. The *Catechism* tells us, "Christ is thus really and mysteriously made *present*." (1357)

The Eucharist finds its beginning when Jesus instituted it at the Last Supper. Jesus Christ instructed, "Do this in remembrance of me." (Lk 22:19; 1 Cor 11:24-25) Jesus also asked His disciples to accept this great gift of His sacramental presence and to repeat it until He returned — "until he comes" (1 Cor 11:26) Thank God for the great GIFT and miracle of Jesus present in the Blessed Sacrament!

Saint Faustina and the Eucharist

Saint Faustina stated, "All the good that is in me is due to Holy Communion."[165] This humble soul derived much strength from receiving Jesus in Holy Communion. One time she neatly etched in her *Diary,* "When my strength begins to fail, it is Holy Communion that will sustain me and give me strength. Indeed, I fear the day on which I would not receive Holy Communion. My soul draws astonishing strength from Holy Communion."[166]

Faustina was well aware of Jesus' presence within her after receiving Holy Communion. She wrote, "Oh, how happy I am to be a dwelling place for You, O Lord! My heart is a temple in which You dwell continually."[167] She also expressed in her *Diary,* "If the angels were capable of envy, they would envy us for two things: one is the receiving of Holy Communion, and the other is suffering."[168]

Saint Faustina's birth name, as we know was Helena Kowalska. When she received her new name in the religious life, it was not just Sr. Maria Faustina Kowalska. Her name was actually, "Sister Maria Faustina Kowalska of the Most Blessed Sacrament." The young nun was deeply connected with the Blessed Sacrament.

In fact, Sr. Faustina was madly in love with Jesus in the Blessed Sacrament. You might recall that she used to sing Eucharistic hymns to the children for whom she cared. Jesus was always on her mind. Perhaps unknowingly, she passed along her love of our Eucharistic Lord through her songs! As we learned earlier, Aldona was moved by Helena's hymns.

In religious life, Faustina spent all of her time speaking to Jesus and consoling His Sacred Heart. Of course, she never neglected her duties in doing so. Through much prayer and a gift from God, our friend Faustina eventually became united to Jesus. So, in a sense, her thoughts were His thoughts and His thoughts were hers, as Sr. Faustina contemplated Jesus' great Love and Mercy and as Jesus worked through His holy daughter Faustina.

The humble nun expressed about her union with Jesus, "Our hearts are constantly united. Though outwardly I am distracted by my various duties, the presence of Jesus plunges me constantly in profound recollection."[169]

One time, our friend Faustina expressed in her *Diary,* "After Holy Communion, I felt the beating of the Heart of Jesus in my own heart. Although I have been aware, for a long time, that Holy Communion continues in me until the next Communion, today — and throughout the whole day — I am adoring Jesus in my heart and asking Him, by His grace, to protect little children from the evil that threatens them. A vivid and even physically felt presence of God continues throughout the day and does not in the least interfere with my duties."[170]

There are numerous entries in Faustina's *Diary* that speak of the Blessed Sacrament and Holy Communion. Earlier, I mentioned that a seraphim angel delivered Holy Communion to Sr. Faustina when she was unable to go to the chapel. Many times, Jesus showed to the young mystic visions of the rays of the Divine Mercy emanating from the Sacred Host.

Jesus continually let Faustina in on very holy mysteries in the mystical life. One time He told her, **"But I want to tell you that eternal life must begin already here on earth through Holy Communion. Each Holy Communion makes you more capable of communing with God throughout eternity."**[171] This is very beautiful news indeed! Let us meditate upon this truth from Jesus and prepare to receive Holy Communion more worthily.

Jesus also sadly lamented to His little Faustina that souls pay no attention to Him, even when they receive Him in Holy Communion!

I desire to unite Myself with human souls; My great delight is to unite Myself with souls. Know, My daughter, that when I come to a human heart in Holy Communion, My hands are full of all kinds of graces which I want to give to the soul. But souls do not even pay any attention to Me; they leave Me to Myself and busy themselves with other things. Oh, how sad I am that souls do not recognize Love! They treat Me as a dead object.[172]

Union with Jesus

Sister Faustina spoke of a certain profound peace to be experienced in the spiritual life when a soul is united to God. She explained, "[I]f a soul loves God sincerely and is intimately united with Him, then, even though such a soul may be living in the midst of difficult external circumstances, nothing can disturb its interior life; and in the midst of corruption, it can remain pure and unsullied; because the great love of God gives it strength for battle, and God also protects in a special way, even in a miraculous way, a soul that loves Him sincerely."[173]

In her special union with God, our friend Faustina physically felt His presence. She didn't think anyone could possibly understand it. She wrote, "Love was becoming purer and stronger, and the Lord brought my will into the closest union with His own holy will. No one will understand what I experience in that splendid palace of my soul where I abide constantly with my Beloved. No exterior thing hinders my union with God."[174]

Sister Faustina, sometimes, had trouble explaining the mysteries of God and the experiences in her heart and soul. Under obedience to write in her *Diary*, she did her best to explain her union with Jesus. She wrote: "God approaches a soul in a special way known only to Himself and to the soul. ... Love presides in this union, and everything is achieved by love alone. Jesus gives Himself to the soul in a gentle and sweet manner, and in His depths there is peace. He grants the soul many graces and makes it capable of sharing His eternal thoughts. And frequently, He reveals to it His divine plans."[175]

Saint Faustina received so many graces and gifts meant to glorify God (such as a hidden stigmata, visions, revelations, the gift of contemplation, bilocation, levitation, reading human souls, a gift of prophesy, deep knowledge of God's mercy and of the Blessed Trinity, and mystical espousal). Even with all of these amazing gifts, the humble nun knew what was most important. She said, "Neither graces, nor revelations, nor raptures, nor gifts granted to a soul make it perfect, but rather the intimate union of the soul with God. ... My sanctity and perfection consist in the close union of my will with the will of God."[176]

A secret mystic

Yes, our friend Sr. Faustina, a simple and poorly educated nun of the second choir was actually a secret mystic, entrusted with a great prophetic mission by God. She was often in mystical communion with Jesus and Mary, even as she carried out her duties as if nothing extraordinary was going on inside her.

Her graces and great gifts were only known to her confessors, but occasionally, someone would witness one of them. Then the murmurings would spread throughout the convent and Faustina would be ridiculed. One day, Sr. Kajetana Bartkowiak came to visit Sr. Faustina. When Sr. Faustina didn't answer the door quickly enough, Sr. Kajetana let herself in. Sister Faustina was levitating over her bed, seemingly gazing into the mystical distance. Needless to say, Sr. Kajetana was flabbergasted! Sister Faustina came to and quickly greeted Sr. Kajetana, acting as if nothing out of the ordinary had just occurred. Mother Irena Krzyżanowska got wind of the astonishing occurrence from Sr. Kajetana and forbade her to speak of it.[177]

One time, Jesus told His precious Faustina, **"See, I have left My heavenly throne to become united with you. What you see is just a tiny part and already your soul swoons with love. How amazed will your heart be when you see Me in all My glory."**[178] Can we even imagine this? We can certainly look forward to the amazement of Heaven as we work hard on our journey towards eternal life.

Yes, we are called to become holy! I've said it before but it bears repeating, it is what our time on Earth, our pilgrimage here, is all about — working out our salvation, all the while helping others to do so as well. Jesus told St. Faustina:

> **Let souls who are striving for perfection particularly adore My mercy, because the abundance of graces which I grant them flows from My mercy. I desire that these souls distinguish themselves by boundless trust in My mercy. I myself will attend to the sanctification of such souls. I will provide them with everything they will need to attain sanctity. The graces of My mercy are drawn by means of one vessel only, and that is — trust. The more a soul trusts, the more it will receive. Souls that trust boundlessly are a great comfort to Me, because I pour all the treasures of My graces into them. I rejoice that they ask for much, because it is My desire to give much, very much. On the other**

hand, I am sad when souls ask for little, when they narrow their hearts.[179]

I'll share a quick story with you. During the writing of this book, on a First Saturday, I went to Confession. After I left the confessional, I found a place to kneel in the church to pray and make my penance. As I was praying to Jesus, I thought about His great Mercy to forgive my sins and remembered our Lord's words to our friend Faustina (quoted above), **"Let souls who are striving for perfection particularly adore My mercy, because the abundance of graces which I grant them flows from My mercy."** Kneeling there, I continually adored Jesus in His mercy and prayed over and over, "Jesus, I adore You in Your mercy!" When it was time to leave, I got up from my knees and exited the pew. I genuflected, got up, and was amazed at what I saw. It was a statue of St. Faustina by the window at the end of the pew. I had never seen it there before that moment! It was a comfort to me to see a representation of our friend Faustina to whom Jesus had given the instruction to adore Him in His Mercy.

Indeed, each one of us should strive for perfection in the spiritual life. Jesus promises that when we boundlessly trust Him, He will take care of our sanctification. You might recall here that I have often referred to Jesus as the Divine Physician, Who knows exactly what we need and when we need it. We absolutely need to trust Jesus with our lives.

Spiritual battle

In a chapter devoted to our own souls and the spiritual life, we must touch upon the spiritual battle. For, it's real. It may seem invisible most times, like the angels and demons we mentioned earlier, yet the battle is a reality in our lives. It's not something to fear. Yet, we should be prepared and armed for battle. Let's talk about that.

Just a little while ago, in speaking of union with God, St. Faustina let us in on the fact that being in union with God gives us strength for battle. You see, the battle is no secret. It's a fact of life. Many times throughout her *Diary*, our friend Faustina spoke of her battles with evil and Jesus Himself gave St. Faustina a retreat on spiritual warfare.

Jesus told Sr. Faustina, **"My daughter, I want to teach you about spiritual warfare. Never trust in yourself, but abandon yourself totally to My will. ... I will not delude you with prospects of peace and consolations; on the contrary, prepare for great battles. ... Fight like a knight, so that I can reward you. Do not be unduly fearful, because you are not alone."**[180]

On one hand, this statement from Jesus can give us the chills, fretting about the battle ahead. However, Jesus promises that when we keep our eyes on Him and trust Him by abandoning ourselves totally to His will, there is nothing to fear — He will sustain us. We are never alone.

Saint Paul exhorted in his Letter to the Ephesians:

> Finally, be strong in the Lord and in the strength of his power. Put on the whole armor of God, so that you may be able to stand against the wiles of the devil. For our struggle is not against enemies of blood and flesh, but against the rulers, against the authorities, against the cosmic powers of this present darkness, against the spiritual forces of evil in the heavenly places. Therefore take up the whole armor of God, so that you may be able to withstand on that evil day, and having done everything, to stand firm. Stand therefore, and fasten the belt of truth around your waist, and put on the breastplate of righteousness (Eph 6:10-14).

We just discussed the Sacraments of Holy Communion and Confession. These are powerful aids and protection in our spiritual lives. We can consider them a part of the "armor of God."

Inside scoop on the devil

One day, Sr. Faustina cleverly uncovered some inside scoop from the devil himself! Here's what happened: Our friend Faustina wrote, "I saw Satan hurrying about and looking for someone among the sisters, but he could find no one. I felt an interior inspiration to command him in the Name of God to confess to me what he was looking for among the sisters." Satan unwillingly confessed, "I am looking for idle souls." Once again, Sr. Faustina commanded him in the Name of God to tell her "to which souls in religious life he has the easiest access." The devil confessed, "To lazy and idle souls." Sister Faustina understood that no such souls were there at that time. She wrote, "Let the toiling and tired souls rejoice."[181]

Saint Faustina received a special grace to do what she was inspired to do. While I do not recommend that any one of us speak directly to the devil or demons, we should take Faustina's discovery seriously. In a variety of ways, the devil tries to trip us up and knock us off the path that leads to Heaven. One way is to temp us to idleness. That said, it's never wrong to seek rest when needed, but we should be careful not to simply be lazy about our spiritual lives and vulnerable to the devil's tricks.

The Apostle Paul notes in 2 Thessalonians 3:11;13 the danger of "living in idleness" and being "mere busybodies," as well as issuing a call to "not be weary in doing what is right." My friend and former spiritual director, Fr. John A. Hardon, S.J., used to say often, "There's work to be done!" Let's stay occupied for the Lord, actively loving of God and neighbor, which we can do with prayer and devotion and showing our love with works of mercy.

Choice graces in persevering prayer

Jesus, Mary, and the saints were constantly guiding Sr. Faustina in ways to pray and trust. For now, I will mention just two invaluable surprising facts about prayer which can aid us in the spiritual life. Both were revealed to our friend Faustina by Jesus Himself. Both revelations from Jesus can aid us in persevering in our prayers.

First of all, there is no doubt about it, we all struggle with prayer. No matter how devout, pious, or dedicated we may be. After all, we are only human. We are not angels! Add to that, the evil one does whatever he can to distract us from prayer or keep us too busy with other things (we think we have to do) and then we miss out on valuable time for prayer. And there's also the problem I just mentioned about idleness. Without a healthy prayer life, our soul starts to wither away. We can't let that happen!

Allow me first, to note that there are various forms of prayer and you can read more about them in the *Catechism*. Very simply for now, we can say that we have our public prayer and our private prayer. Many folks may pray together with family and at church and also, we have our own personal prayer life in which we commune with God (hopefully at every opportunity!). You might call to mind Faustina's father Stanislaus's loud bursts of prayerful song every morning. In his case, his personal prayers in a certain way, became a "public" prayer because the family couldn't help but hear him and could join in if they so pleased.

Truth be told, we sometimes get bored at prayer, or our mind races ahead thinking of what we have to do next or unnecessarily worrying about the past. Another problem is that we might fear that our prayers are insignificant. They can sometimes feel as dry as a bone! All of these, of course, are distractions, most likely from "you-know-who," as I call the evil one. We can pray for the graces to push through the difficulties and distractions and continue to pray.

Saint Faustina shared her own personal problems with prayer. "The interior difficulties are discouragement, dryness, heaviness of spirit and temptations. The exterior difficulties are human respect and time; one must observe the time set apart for prayer." She also noted, "... the soul must be patient to persevere in prayer."[182]

Wisdom from the Garden

During a Holy Hour on January 7, 1937, Faustina learned something quite incredible. It helped her soul and it will help ours too. That is, if we heed the lesson. Our friend recalled it in her *Diary*. She wrote, "[T]he Lord allowed me to taste His Passion. I shared in the bitterness of the suffering that filled His soul to overflowing. Jesus gave me to understand how a soul should be faithful to prayer despite torments, dryness, and temptations; because oftentimes the realization of God's great plans depends mainly on such prayer. If we do not persevere in such prayer, we frustrate what the Lord wanted to do through us or within us."

Saint Faustina learned a great revelation. We must persevere in our prayers in order not to interfere with God's holy plans! Our friend, the mystic encourages us: "Let every soul remember these words: 'And being in anguish, He prayed longer.' I always prolong such prayer as much as is in my power and in conformity with my duty."[183] Let's take a moment and ponder Jesus praying in the Garden before His arrest and subsequent scourging and crucifixion. He was suffering very much, and as Scripture tells us, He was in *agony*. What did He do? Did He give up? No! He continued praying. He persevered! His example and His graces for us will give us strength to persevere in our own prayers and in our lives.

Another time, St. Faustina noted in her *Diary*, "There are times in life when the soul finds comfort only in profound prayer. Would that souls knew how to persevere in prayer at such times. This is very important."[184]

Jesus reserves great graces for later!

When we might be tempted to give up on prayer — we feel we are too busy to pray longer (or too lazy!) — let's consider something hugely important that Jesus revealed to His daughter Faustina. She had been making a Holy Hour. Well, she was trying to! It began "with great difficulty." She was distracted with "a certain yearning," and her "mind was dimmed," as well, she "could not understand the simplest forms of prayer." So, what would have been a Holy Hour of prayer was instead, an hour "of struggle" according to our friend. So, Faustina resolved to pray a second hour. Her "inner sufferings increased." She experienced "great dryness and discouragement." Most of us would give up by now. What did Faustina do?

"I resolved," she said, "to pray for a third hour." During this hour, St. Faustina resolved to kneel "without any support."

Her body started to "clamor for rest." Faustina earnestly pushed her will to continue, stretching out her arms and not even speaking. She recalled, "I persisted by sheer will." She continued her resolve as the third hour ticked away. The determined sister began to speak to Jesus of her vows to Him, pointing out her ring to Him. Her heart was then "inundated with a wave of love." God's presence pervaded her soul.

During that time, much happened between Jesus and His bride. He appeared to her in a vision of being stripped and beaten. Faustina saw "His eyes flooded with tears and blood, His face disfigured and covered with spittle." Jesus let her know that she must resemble her Betrothed, that His love for human souls caused Him great suffering, and that He finds repose in her heart. He then enlightened Faustina with profound words.

Jesus said, "**I often wait with great graces until the end of prayer**."[185] We should let these profound and enlightening words sink in to our hearts. Saint Faustina had painfully struggled in prayer, yet, she persisted, and Jesus rewarded her determined love with the gift of Himself, in communing with her and letting her know that He found comfort in her heart. "**Your heart is My repose**," He said.

Let us remember too that Jesus taught Faustina that giving up on prayer interferes with God's holy plans to work in us and through us. So, let's not think our prayers are insignificant any longer. Our Lord desires these prayers. Also, let us remember that Jesus revealed to Faustina that He often reserves the great graces until the end of prayer. Let us keep going!

Getting ready to meet our Maker

Saint Faustina meditated often on life and death, and God's unfathomable Love and Mercy. She titled her reflection, "The Soul's Expectation of the Coming of the Lord" and recorded it in her *Diary*:

> I do not know, O Lord, at what hour You will come.
> And so I keep constant watch and listen
> As Your chosen bride,

Knowing that You like to come unexpected,
Yet, a pure heart will sense You from afar, O Lord.

I wait for You, Lord, in calm and silence,
With great longing in my heart
And with invincible desire.
I feel that my love for You is changing into fire,
And that it will rise up to heaven like a flame at life's end,
And then all my wishes will be fulfilled.

Come then, at last, my most sweet Lord
And take my thirsting heart
There, to Your home in the lofty regions of heaven,
Where Your eternal life perdures.

Life on this earth is but an agony,
As my heart feels it is created for the heights.
For it the lowlands of this life hold no interest,
For my homeland is in heaven — this I firmly believe.[186]

Whatever age we may be, we too, should reflect upon our lives and on eternal life. During the time gifted to us during our life on this planet Earth, we should do all we can to please God and help many souls to Heaven. One way to help souls is by praying the Chaplet of Divine Mercy for them. We will see more about the Chaplet in our final chapter.

Jesus gives us such encouraging promises. He told St. Faustina, **"At the hour of their death, I defend as My own glory every soul that will say this chaplet; or when others say it for a dying person, the pardon is the same. When this chaplet is said by the bedside of a dying person, God's anger is placated, unfathomable mercy envelops the soul, and the very depths of My tender mercy are moved for the sake of the sorrowful Passion of My Son."**[187]

Saint Faustina was a faithful servant of our Lord. In the end, her body was ravaged with tuberculosis. She bravely and prayerfully went home to the Lord on October 5, 1938, at 10:45 p.m. She was only 33 years old. Just like Jesus when He died! Her funeral took place on the First Friday of the month and on the Feast of Our Lady of the Rosary. We should take note that the day of her funeral, a few days after her death is significant — First Friday in honor of the Sacred Heart of Jesus and it was the Feast of Our Lady of the Rosary. All of her life, Jesus and Mary were so important to the humble Polish farm girl, turned nun, and even in death and at her funeral when her body was put to rest. This humble soul is now recognized as one the greatest mystics in the whole history of the Church!

Love for souls burns in Jesus' Heart

Jesus expressed to St. Faustina that love burns in His Heart for souls. He also disclosed a powerful prayer to her. This is how our friend Faustina expressed it in her *Diary*:

> "Today Jesus said to me, **I desire that you know more profoundly the love that burns in My Heart for souls, and you will understand this when you meditate upon My Passion. Call upon My mercy on behalf of sinners; I desire their salvation. When you say this prayer, with a contrite heart and with faith on behalf of some sinner, I will give him the grace of conversion. This is the prayer: O Blood and Water, which gushed forth from the Heart of Jesus as a fount of Mercy for us, I trust in You.**"[188]

We can pray this simple, yet profound prayer too. We can pray it at any time. It's good to commit it to memory. Before I go to sleep each night, I pray it over and over for each member of my family and anyone I feel who could use prayer.

Chosen Souls

Jesus revealed to St. Faustina His chosen souls and how they transform the world. **"Chosen souls are, in My hand, lights which I cast into the darkness of the world and with which I illumine it. As stars illumine the night, so chosen souls illumine the earth. And the more perfect a soul is, the stronger and the more far-reaching is the light shed by it. It can be hidden and unknown, even to those closest to it, and yet** its holiness is reflected in souls even to the most distant extremities of the world."[189]

Though His chosen souls are few, they actually sustain the world! He said, **"Your great trust in Me forces Me to continuously grant you graces."**[190] He also said:

"[T]here are souls living in the world who love Me dearly. I dwell in their hearts with delight. But they are few. In convents too, there are souls that fill My Heart with joy. They bear My features … . Their number is very small. They are a defense for the world before the justice of the Heavenly Father and a means of obtaining mercy for the world. The love and sacrifice of these souls sustain the world in existence."[191]

We should ponder this reality and pray that we can also become pleasing to Jesus in our wholehearted trust in Him so that by God's grace, our souls will illuminate the world.

Sometimes, we might feel that we are not accomplishing much at all due to various circumstances, responsibilities, and pulls on our attention. But, let us be encouraged by Jesus' words to Faustina. He said, **"Know, my daughter, that your silent, day-to-day martyrdom in complete submission to My will ushers many souls into heaven. And when it seems to you that your suffering exceeds your strength, contemplate My wounds."**[192]

This is wonderful news! When we are obedient to our state of life, Jesus can usher many souls to Heaven. Keep your chin up! Keep praying and striving to be close to Jesus, Mary, and the saints!

Something to Think About

Take a few moments to ponder what you have learned. Consider Jesus' words to His "Secretary of Divine Mercy." He instructed:

> **[L]et three virtues adorn you in a particular way: humility, purity of intention and love. Do nothing beyond what I demand of you, and accept everything that My hand gives you. Strive for a life of recollection so that you can hear My voice, which is so soft that only recollected souls can hear it...**[193]

Will you strive to follow Jesus' instructions? Can you pause before responding to all that comes to you and be sure that your intentions are filled with love and purity? In addition, can you try to accept God's holy will for your life — day-by-day? Will you take more time to recollect your soul and actually carve out times to pray and meditate?

In addition, Jesus told His daughter Faustina, "**Strive for a life of recollection so that you can hear My voice, which is so soft that only recollected souls can hear it.**"[194] Take those words to your own heart.

Finally, remember, Jesus asks that we meditate upon His Passion and adore Him in His Mercy. Let's do that often.

 Pray

Dear Jesus and Mary, please guide me. Jesus, I trust in You! I want to praise You forever for Your great Mercy! Dear St. Faustina, please pray for me.

 A Merciful Action

Pray for those who are away from God. Consider doing a penance for them.

The Divine Mercy Image is a great source
of comfort and hope for all.

11

Divine Mercy for the World

Our world certainly needs God's unfathomable loving Mercy. It always has and it always will. We are greatly blessed that God raised up St. Faustina to proclaim that God is Love and Mercy! Saint John Paul II stated during the Holy Mass for the Consecration of the Shrine of Divine Mercy, in Kraków-Łagiewniki, Poland, (August 17, 2002), "How greatly today's world needs God's mercy! In every continent, from the depth of human suffering, a cry for mercy seems to rise up."[195]

Holy Scripture has always spoken to us of God's Mercy. "All the paths of the Lord are steadfast love and faithfulness" (Ps 25:10). "His compassion is over all that he has made" (Ps 145:9). Our Lord refers to Himself as, "merciful and gracious, slow to anger, and abounding in steadfast love" (Ex 34:6; cf. Ps 103:8 and Joel 2:13).

For some time though, the revealed truth of Divine Mercy had seemingly faded into the background of the Church's life and teaching. Blessed Fr. Michael Sopoćko found this to be true and searched the writings of the Fathers of the Church for proof that Faustina's claim that mercy is God's greatest attribute. He was pleased to find similar statements in St. Fulgentius, St. Idelphonse, St. Thomas Aquinas, and St. Augustine, who, in commenting on the Psalms had much to say on Divine Mercy, "calling it indeed the greatest of God's attributes."[196]

Later on, renowned experts in the spirituality of St. Faustina, namely: Robert Stackpole, STD, Very Rev. Kazimierz Chwalek, MIC, provincial superior of the Congregation of Marian Fathers of the Immaculate Conception; and Rev. Seraphim Michalenko, MIC, vice-postulator of the Cause for the Canonization of St.

Maria Faustina Kowalska have concluded that we cannot "over-estimate the importance of the recovery of the centrality of God's merciful love to the life and mission of the Church — a recovery to which St. Faustina made such a major contribution."[197] Pope John Paul II, Pope Benedict XVI, and Pope Francis have all spoken about Divine Mercy and have all confirmed the centrality of the message of Divine Mercy.

Jesus told St. Faustina, **"My Heart rejoices in this title of Mercy. Proclaim that mercy is the greatest attribute of God. All the works of My hands are crowned with mercy."**[198]

"Tell all souls"

Jesus also told His Secretary of Divine Mercy, **"Tell souls not to place within their own hearts obstacles to My mercy, which so greatly wants to act within them. My mercy works in all those hearts which open their doors to it. Both the sinner and the righteous person have need of My mercy. Conversion, as well as perseverance, is a grace of My mercy."**[199]

Jesus calls us to turn to Him — to trust Him, to turn away from sin and accept His amazing Mercy for our souls. After that, He calls us to impart His Mercy to others. We might hesitate. We might feel inept or unqualified. We might be afraid to move beyond our comfort zones.

If we pause to consider some of the greatest saints (including St. Faustina), we will recognize that every one of them at some point might have felt unqualified to spread God's Love and Mercy to the world. Some were uneducated, unskilled, or frail. Yet, they moved forward in Faith (most times beyond their comfort zones!). And God equipped them! It's the same with you and me. We can pray for the graces to be a light to others by imparting God's Mercy and teaching others about it.

This can unfold in a variety of ways. Mother Teresa was famous for saying, "Love begins at home." We start our love there with our prayerful good deeds. We can pray to be a light of love and mercy to those in our own families. And if God allows (and He usually does!), we broaden our reach to others. Below, we will discuss the degrees of mercy as Jesus taught Faustina.

These are ways to show God's love and mercy.

There will also be times in our lives when we can teach others about God's Divine Mercy. Perhaps even to a complete stranger. We can gift a copy of this book to someone we want to enlighten about Divine Mercy. I also recommend literature and material from the Marian Fathers, who are the official translators of the *Diary*. We can pray to learn ways we can help others. It's important to try to be attentive to the needs of others. There's no need to feel overwhelmed about this task of imparting mercy. Most times, it occurs one-on-one within everyday encounters and simple conversations.

Mother Mary's warning

We touched upon the Blessed Mother's words earlier in our chapter on Mary. However, it is important to repeat them here. Saint Faustina made sure to note in her *Diary* about the Blessed Mother's visit with important instructions and a sober warning. On March 26, 1936, Faustina was meditating and felt God's presence envelop her in a special way.

Black ink flowing from her pen, the young mystic later entered her experience in the *Diary*:

> Then I saw the Mother of God, who said to me, *Oh, how pleasing to God is the soul that follows faithfully the inspirations of His grace! I gave the Savior to the world; as for you, you have to speak to the world about His great mercy and prepare the world for the Second Coming of Him who will come, not as a merciful Savior, but as a just Judge. Oh, how terrible is that day! Determined is the day of justice, the day of divine wrath. The angels tremble before it. Speak to souls about this great mercy while it is still the time for* [granting] *mercy. If you keep silent now, you will be answering for a great number of souls on that terrible day. Fear nothing. Be faithful to the end. I sympathize with you.*[200]

We all need to heed Mother Mary's warning. She deeply desires that all her children be one day safe in Heaven for all eternity. Mary told Faustina that God is very pleased with souls who follow Him and respond to His grace! In addition, she did not hesitate to tell her that a terrible day of justice will come when Jesus returns as the Just Judge.

As we know, St. Faustina was entrusted with the great responsibility of spreading the message of Divine Mercy. She was young and struggled with the huge task and with trying to figure out how she could accomplish it. She didn't give up. She trusted God.

We too, need to do our own part to spread the message of God's Divine Mercy. Mary's sobering words should spring us into action with regard to getting our lives in order and helping others to do the same.

Let's delve into the Image of the Divine Mercy and all of its components, as well as the five parts of the message.

The Divine Mercy Image

First of all, as a reminder, it was at the Congregation of Our Lady of the Sisters of Mercy in Płock on February 22, 1931, that Jesus appeared to Sr. Faustina when she was in her cell. As we discussed earlier, He appeared to her in the vision of The Divine Mercy and asked the unsuspecting and amazed young nun to have it painted. He told her the signature line should be, **"Jesus, I trust in You."** He said, **"I desire that this image be venerated, first in your chapel, and then throughout the world."**[201]

Saint Faustina was instructed by Jesus to propagate this devotion, to make sure that the image was painted, and to make sure that the Sunday following Easter would be dedicated to Divine Mercy Sunday when Mercy and graces abound! But how difficult it was for her to carry out Jesus' requests! She was not believed and had to persevere patiently and wait for a spiritual director who could guide her, and so much more.

Even after her superiors approved of moving forward with a painting, there was much trouble in getting someone to do the actual painting. Finally, Fr. Sopoćko hired the first artist to paint the image. Saint Faustina recalled her initial sadness over the way the painting was coming along.

She recorded in her *Diary*:

Once, when I was visiting the artist [Eugene Kazimirowski] who was painting the image, and saw that it was not as beautiful as Jesus is, I felt very sad about it, but I hid this deep in my heart. When we had left the artist's house, Mother Superior [Irene] stayed in town to attend to some matters while I returned home alone. I went immediately to the chapel and wept a good deal. I said to the Lord, "Who will paint You as beautiful as You are?" Then I heard these words: **Not in the beauty of the color, nor of the brush lies the greatness of this image, but in My grace.**[202]

Divine Mercy Image elements

As we discuss the Divine Mercy Image and the various elements of it, as well as Jesus' promises, we will better understand just how powerful and meaningful the Divine Mercy Image really is. With regard to the image, Jesus said: **"I promise that the soul that will venerate this image will not perish. I also promise victory over [its] enemies already here on earth, especially at the hour of death. I Myself will defend it as My own glory."**[203] We need to bring the image to the dying!

The image is powerful! It is like a Living Icon — it holds the entire Paschal mystery within it. Countless conversions have occurred through the Image of Divine Mercy. Jesus Himself works through the image. I note some of these miracles in my books on Divine Mercy. One example is about a young woman who was very far away from God and suddenly dropped to her knees in a major conversion after seeing the Image of Divine Mercy on a little prayer leaflet given to her by her mother! She remained kneeling in the same spot for 4 hours, crying out to Jesus! Her entire life was transformed. She grew up, she married, had eight children — and two are nuns. And in God's wonderful providence, this woman became close with Saint Padre Pio!

The Divine Mercy Image is a great source of comfort and hope for all. Jesus disclosed that His Divine Mercy Image would draw many souls back to His Love and Mercy and would be a protection for those who dwelled in the shelter of the rays emitting from His Merciful Heart. Jesus also described the image as a "Vessel of Graces" to which people could come to and seek His Love and Mercy.

One of the main purposes of The Divine Mercy Image is to be a "Vessel of Graces" for everyone. Jesus revealed when we pray before the Image of Divine Mercy, we are praying in the actual presence of Jesus. This is extremely amazing and comforting!

There are some significant parts to the image. I'll briefly mention the significance of the parts:

Jesus' Eyes: Jesus said: **"My gaze from this image is like My gaze from the cross."**[204] Saint Faustina made sure to point out to the artist and to Fr. Sopoćko that Jesus' eyes are to be gazing downwards and towards us.

His Hands: Jesus' right hand is held in a gesture of blessing. When we pray before the Image of Divine Mercy we should ask Jesus to bless us, our family and friends, our community, our country, the Church, and the whole world. Jesus desires to grant great graces to souls everywhere.

The Rays: Rays are coming from Jesus' Merciful Heart. At first, St. Faustina's spiritual director, Fr. Sopoćko, was unclear about the meaning of the rays. He asked Faustina to ask Jesus for an explanation. Jesus revealed to her, **"The two rays denote Blood and Water. The pale ray stands for the Water which makes souls righteous. The red ray stands for the Blood which is the life of souls... These two rays issued forth from the very depths of My tender mercy when My agonized Heart was opened by a lance on the Cross. These rays shield souls from the wrath of My Father. Happy is the one who will dwell in their shelter, for the just hand of God shall not lay hold of him."**[205]

His Heart: We know from St. Faustina's *Diary* that Jesus revealed to her that though the Heart of Jesus is not actually visible in the Image as shown to St. Faustina in Płock, His Heart is the same as in the devotion to the Sacred Heart for Jesus showed it to her. Jesus also told St. Faustina:

From all My wounds, like from streams, mercy flows for souls, but the wound in My Heart is the fountain of unfathomable mercy. From this fountain spring all graces for souls. The flames of compassion burn Me. I desire greatly to pour them out upon souls. Speak to the whole world about My mercy.[206]

His Feet: The position of Jesus' feet in the image is important. Saint Faustina stated that one can see the wounds from the nails on His feet and that His left foot was more forward than the right foot, which meant Jesus was coming to us, with His Divine Mercy.

Jesus appeared in His Divine Mercy Image to St. Faustina others times, in addition to the first time (February 22, 1931). For instance, on October 26, 1934, St. Faustina saw a vision of Jesus in The Divine Mercy. He appeared above the chapel in Vilnius when she was walking with the students. The rays from Jesus' Divine Mercy Image enveloped the chapel of the Congregation and the infirmary of the students. Then the rays spread over the entire world. Many other times, Jesus showed St. Faustina Himself in His Image of Divine Mercy making a Sign of the Cross and blessing with His right hand.

Five parts of the Divine Mercy message

Through Saint Faustina, Jesus has taught us the beautiful Gospel of Divine Mercy. God's unfathomable Mercy and Love which has always existed, but through Jesus' teachings to our friend Faustina, our modern world can better understand. Through the five parts of the Divine Mercy Message, we can experience Divine Mercy.

They are easy to remember by the acronym F.I.N.C.H.:

- The Feast
- The Image
- The Novena
- The Chaplet
- The Hour of Great Mercy.

With regard to the Feast of Divine Mercy, Jesus said: "**I desire that the Feast of Mercy be a refuge and shelter for all souls, and especially for poor sinners. On that day the very depths of My tender mercy are open. I pour out a whole ocean of graces upon those souls who approach the fount of My Mercy. The soul that will go to Confession and receive Holy Communion shall obtain complete forgiveness of sins and punishment. On that day all the divine floodgates through which grace flow are opened. Let no soul fear to draw near to Me, even though its sins be as scarlet.**"[207]

Our friend, Faustina was blessed to learn some of the fruits of the message of Divine Mercy before she finally closed her eyes to her life on Earth. On November 10, 1937, Mother Irene showed to Sr. Faustina, a booklet which contained the Chaplet, the Litany, and the Novena to The Divine Mercy, along with the image. As Faustina glanced through it, Jesus told her, "**Already there are many souls who have been drawn to My love by this image. My mercy acts in souls through this work.**" What a beautiful consolation this must have been for Sister Faustina, who wrote, "I learned that many souls had experienced God's grace."[208]

Divine Mercy Chaplet

Jesus told St. Faustina, "**Through the chaplet you will obtain everything, if what you ask for will be compatible with My will.**"[209] The Chaplet of Divine Mercy is a powerful prayer which Jesus taught to St. Faustina. It can be prayed any time. Jesus specifically asked that it be recited as a novena. He promised, "**By this novena** [of Chaplets]**, I will grant every possible grace to souls.**"[210] The Chaplet is especially efficacious in praying for the dying. You will find the instructions for praying the Divine Mercy Chaplet in the Appendix of Prayers in the back of this book.

How did the powerful prayer of the Divine Mercy Chaplet come about? Here's what happened: On the evening of September 13, 1935, St. Faustina was in her cell and saw a vision of an angel clad in "a dazzling robe," who was, "the executor of divine wrath." He had been sent to Earth to punish for sins. From a cloud, "bolts of thunder and flashes of lightening were springing into his hands." Faustina wanted to implore the angel to hold off, even for a few minutes, hoping the world could somehow do penance. She found her plea to be "a mere nothing in the face of the divine anger." However, Faustina saw the Most Holy Trinity and also felt the power of Jesus' grace in her soul. She "was instantly snatched up before the Throne of God."

Interiorly, Faustina heard the prayer of the Divine Mercy Chaplet and immediately prayed it, earnestly pleading to God for the world. By this powerful prayer, the angel was rendered helpless to carry out the intended punishment. Faustina recalled, "Never before had I prayed with such inner power as I did then."[211]

The next day, Jesus showed His daughter Faustina how to pray the Chaplet and explained its importance. He said: **"Every time you enter the chapel, immediately recite the prayer which I taught you yesterday."** St. Faustina recalled, "When I had said the prayer, in my soul I heard these words: **This prayer will serve to appease My wrath. You will recite it for nine days, on the beads of the rosary, in the following manner: First of all, you will say one OUR FATHER and HAIL MARY and the I BELIEVE IN GOD. Then on the OUR FATHER beads you will say the following words: 'Eternal Father, I offer You the Body and Blood, Soul and Divinity of Your dearly beloved Son, Our Lord Jesus Christ, in atonement for our sins and those of the whole world.' On the HAIL MARY beads you will say the following words: 'For the sake of His sorrowful Passion have mercy on us and on the whole world.' In conclusion, three times you will recite these words: 'Holy God, Holy Mighty One, Holy Immortal One, have mercy on us and on the whole world.'"[212]**

Jesus, later announced many promises for praying the Chaplet with trust. Saint Faustina often prayed the Chaplet beside the dying or for the dying located somewhere else, and even to ask for much needed rain and to stop a storm.

Saint Faustina recalled praying the Divine Mercy Chaplet for a dying soul. She had been awakened one night and had become aware of the dying soul who sought her prayers. She asked Jesus for grace for the soul.

She wrote:

The following afternoon, when I entered the ward, I saw someone dying, and learned that the agony had started during the night. When I verified it — it had been at the time when I had been asked for prayer. And just then, I heard a voice in my soul: **Say the chaplet which I taught you.** I ran to fetch my rosary and knelt down by the dying person and, with all the ardor of my soul, I began to say the chaplet. Suddenly the dying person opened her eyes and looked at me; I had not managed to finish the entire chaplet when she died, with extraordinary peace. I fervently asked the Lord to fulfill the promise He had given me for the recitation of the chaplet. The Lord gave me to know that the soul had been granted the grace He had promised me. That was the first soul to receive the benefit of the Lord's promise. I could feel the power of mercy envelop that soul.[213]

Later on, St. Faustina heard these words, **"At the hour of their death, I defend as My own glory every soul that will say this chaplet; or when others say it for a dying person, the pardon is the same. When this chaplet is said by the bedside of a dying person, God's anger is placated, unfathomable mercy envelops the soul, and the very depths of My tender mercy are moved for the sake of the sorrowful Passion of My Son."**[214]

Father Sopoćko, in 1937, obtained the imprimatur for the Chaplet and arranged for its publication in Kraków, along with the Images of The Divine Mercy. The Chaplet of Divine Mercy has spread throughout the world and is the most popular prayer to the Divine Mercy. It has been published in many countries and translated into numerous languages. The Marian priests have worked extensively in circulating material about the message of Divine Mercy throughout the world. Incidentally, St. John Paul II made note of the Chaplet of Divine Mercy at the end of the Act of Entrusting the World to the Divine Mercy.

Immediately after World War II, to promote the teaching of Divine Mercy given by Jesus to St. Faustina, Fr. Józef Andrasz, SJ (Faustina's spiritual director in Kraków) prepared a prayer book titled *Miłosierdzie Boże, ufamy Tobie* (*Divine Mercy, We trust in You*). It played a huge role in promoting the devotion to the Divine Mercy. First published by Jesuits in Kraków, an English version was followed up by the Marians in the United States. Through the work of the Marians, the book spread through Canada, Australia, New Zealand, Asia, and Africa. Later on, it was translated to Spanish and spread throughout Latin America (El Salvador, Colombia, Ecuador, Chile, Mexico, Argentina, Uruguay, Peru and Guatemala) in huge numbers. The prayer book was also distributed in Portuguese in Brazil. In Europe, it was also published in German, Italian, Spanish, and Portuguese.

The three o'clock hour

Jesus told Faustina:

> I remind you, My daughter, that as often as you hear the clock strike the third hour, immerse yourself completely in My mercy, adoring and glorifying it; invoke its omnipotence for the whole world, and particularly for poor sinners; for at that moment mercy was opened wide for every soul. In this hour you can obtain everything for yourself and for others for the asking; it was the hour of grace for the whole world — mercy triumphed over justice.
>
> My daughter, try your best to make the Stations of the Cross in this hour, provided that your duties permit it; and if you are not able to make the Stations of the Cross, then at least step into the chapel for a moment and adore, in the Blessed Sacrament, My Heart, which is full of mercy; and should you be unable to step into the chapel, immerse yourself in prayer there where you happen to be, if only for a very brief instant. I claim veneration for My mercy from every creature, but above

all from you, since it is to you that I have given the most profound understanding of this mystery.[215]

Divine Mercy Novena of Chaplets

A novena is a prayer, typically prayed for nine days in preparation of a celebration of a feast day or to invoke intercession from a particular saint. As we know, St. Faustina prayed many novenas. A novena can be prayed at any time when seeking Heavenly intercession. Jesus specifically asked for the nine-day Divine Mercy Novena to begin on Good Friday and lead up to Divine Mercy Sunday.

For each of the nine days of the novena, Jesus gave St. Faustina specific intentions. They are for: 1) All mankind, especially sinners; 2) the souls of priests and religious; 3) all devout and faithful souls; 4) those who do not believe in God and those who do not yet know Jesus; 5) the souls who have separated themselves from the Church; 6) the meek and humble souls and the souls of little children; 7) the souls who especially venerate and glorify His mercy; 8) the souls detained in purgatory; and 9) souls who have become lukewarm.

Jesus said, **"I desire that during these nine days you bring souls to the fountain of My mercy, that they may draw therefrom strength and refreshment and whatever grace they need in the hardships of life, and especially at the hour of death."**[216]

Degrees of Mercy

Saint Faustina prayed, "Help me, O Lord, that my hands may be merciful and filled with good deeds, so that I may do only good to my neighbors and take upon myself the more difficult and toilsome tasks."[217]

Jesus made very clear to St. Faustina that we are to seek His Mercy, but we are also to impart His great Love and Mercy to others. We learn in Scripture:

> What good is it, my brothers and sisters, if you say you have faith but do not have works? Can faith save you?

If a brother or sister is naked and lacks daily food, and one of you says to them, "Go in peace; keep warm and eat your fill," and yet you do not supply their bodily needs, what is the good of that? So faith by itself, if it has no works, is dead. (Jas 2:14-17)

A big part of Sr. Faustina's and the other sisters' works of mercy included the care of the wards, whom the Congregation took in to help rehabilitate. The girls and women were blessed to have the opportunity of being taught by the kind nuns. As mentioned earlier, the sisters actually worked with them to rescue their souls. Saint Faustina often took a ward under her wing. Her loving and prayerful example were a great comfort and benefit to the girls.

For example, once, while Sr. Faustina was at work in the convent's kitchen, a certain headstrong girl was assigned as her assistant. No one else wanted to work with the girl since she was of a very disagreeable disposition. Sister Faustina could have simply taught the girl how to help out in the kitchen. However, her deep desire to help others always came into play.

Eventually, side-by-side among the pots and pans, Sr. Faustina's holy influence made a wonderful impression on her. Mother Serafina Kukulska, the superior of the convent in Walendow at that time later said that the girl had a transformation beyond recognition! We shouldn't be surprised. The girl was guided by a saint! We too, can be an amazing influence on others when we allow Christ's light to shine through us.

Jesus' instructions

Jesus was very clear when He taught Sr. Faustina the Degrees of Mercy. He told her, **"My daughter, if I demand through you that people revere My mercy, you should be the first to distinguish yourself by this confidence in My mercy. I demand from you deeds of mercy, which are to arise out of love for Me. You are to show mercy to your neighbors always and everywhere. You must not shrink from this or try to excuse or absolve yourself from it."**[218]

We notice that Jesus told her that she had no excuse for not doing the "deeds of mercy." He said, "**always and everywhere**." It's really what our lives should be as Christians. We are to show mercy to others. Jesus is specific with how we are to carry out these deeds or works of mercy.

Jesus said, "**I am giving you three ways of exercising mercy toward your neighbor: the first — by deed, the second — by word, the third — by prayer. In these three degrees is contained the fullness of mercy, and it is an unquestionable proof of love for Me. By this means a soul glorifies and pays reverence to My mercy.**"[219]

We cannot always show mercy in deed due to various circumstances. However, we should try our best to do so when we are able. It's not too difficult to show mercy by word — to encourage someone or to pray with them, or offer our prayers. Another example would be to reach out to someone who is having a difficult time. At times, it might be in helping a complete stranger we meet when out and about. We see they are in some distress and we kindly speak to them. Our presence to them could very well be the dose of holy medicine they need. The opportunities to show mercy by word are endless. Certainly, we can always pray for others as a form of God's Mercy. In addition to our regular prayers, importantly, we need to take time to pray for our enemies and those who have done harm to us.

The Mercy Pope

Divine Mercy deeply touched St. John Paul II's heart. Saint John Paul II believed spreading the message of Divine Mercy was his greatest calling. He initially learned of St. Faustina's Divine Mercy revelations when he was Karol Wojtyla, a young seminarian in Kraków. Drawn to the message of Divine Mercy, as a priest, Karol often visited the convent where St. Faustina had lived. There, he prayed and held retreats. Still later, as Archbishop of Kraków, he led the effort to get St. Faustina's name known before the Congregation for the Causes of Saints. He later defended her cause when Rome questioned the validity of her claims.

During the most difficult years of the Second World War, St. John Paul II was supported by the message of Divine Mercy which was an unending source of hope for him and countless others.

On November 30, 1980, Pope John Paul II published his second encyclical, *Dives in misericordia* ("Rich in mercy"). The following year, an assassination on the pope was attempted. While still recovering from the bullet wounds, that year, Pope John Paul II visited The Shrine of Merciful Love in Collevalenza, Todi, Italy.

He said, "A year ago I published the encyclical *Dives in misericordia*. This circumstance made me come to the Sanctuary of Merciful Love today. By my presence I wish to reconfirm, in a way, the message of that encyclical. I wish to read it again and deliver it again. Right from the beginning of my ministry in St. Peter's See in Rome, I considered this message my special task. Providence has assigned it to me in the present situation of man, the Church, and the world. It could be said that precisely this situation assigned that message to me as my task before God."[220]

When it came time for St. Faustina's beatification on April 18, 1993, Pope John Paul II was to do the honors. He expressed his happiness over the spread of the Divine Mercy message. "Her mission continues and is yielding astonishing fruit. It is truly marvelous how her devotion to the merciful Jesus is spreading in our contemporary world and gaining so many human hearts!"[221] We will see in a little while that he also canonized St. Faustina.

Spark

I mentioned the word, "spark" at the very beginning of St. Faustina's story. I now wish to share Saint John Paul II's words on his last pilgrimage to his homeland Poland, culminating a remarkable journey and when the frail pope consecrated the Divine Mercy Basilica (August 17, 2002) and also entrusted the world to God's Mercy.

Today, therefore, in this Shrine (sic), I wish *solemnly to entrust the world to Divine Mercy*. I do so with the burning desire that the message of God's merciful love, proclaimed here through Saint Faustina, *may be made known to all the peoples of the earth* and fill their hearts with hope. May this message radiate from this place to our beloved homeland and throughout the world. May the binding promise of the Lord Jesus be fulfilled: from here there must go forth "the spark which will prepare the world for his final coming" (cf. *Diary*, 1732).

This spark needs to be lighted by the grace of God. This fire of mercy needs to be passed on to the world. *In the mercy of God the world will find peace and mankind will find happiness*! I entrust this task to you, dear Brothers and Sisters, to the Church in Kraków and Poland, and to all the votaries of Divine Mercy who will come here from Poland and from throughout the world. *May you be witnesses to mercy*![222]

Beatification

As a brief backdrop, a beatification comes before canonization. However, before anyone can be beatified by the Catholic Church, a thorough process of investigation is carried out. In addition, an indisputable miracle has to have occurred due to the intercession of the person. It's not an easy process. We can be assured that when the Church beatifies or canonizes a person who has died, there is not even a shadow of a doubt about the validity of its conclusion.

Certainly, Heaven is populated by saints, but not all have been officially canonized. Not every saint in Heaven has been through the process of investigation and raised to the altar in the Catholic Church to be proclaimed a saint. Many saints lived very quiet lives. Nonetheless, God knows every single saint in Heaven and He has personally opened Heaven's gates for them to live eternally with Him in happiness.

In the case of beatification, first of all, the process cannot begin until five years has passed since the holy individual has passed away. The Supreme Pontiff can waive this waiting period if he deems it appropriate. Next, a bishop of the person's diocese can petition the Holy See to open the cause. If there is no objection, the person's life and virtues are investigated, private and public writings are studied, testimony is gathered to see if the person has practiced heroic virtues in their lifetime.

The person gains the title of "Servant of God" because of this process. The investigation can take many years. Results are reported to the Congregation for the Causes of the Saints. Then, many recommendations are communicated to various parts of the Congregation. There is a vote to determine the person's heroic virtues. Once that is recognized by the Pope, the person gains the title of "Venerable."

The remaining step to the process is that a miracle is approved. And "evidence of the intercessory power of the Venerable Servant of God and thus of his or her union after death with God."[223] In addition, "The scientific commission must determine by accepted scientific criteria that there is no natural explanation for the alleged miracle."[224]

And there's even more! So you can see, it is a complicated process involving many parts and many people to ultimately conclude with a "Blessed" person on their way to becoming declared a saint. That is, after one more miracle is proven.

On April 18, 1993, Pope John Paul II beatified the Venerable Servant of God Sister Maria Faustina Kowalska in Rome on the first Sunday after Easter, Divine Mercy Sunday. Pope John Paul II began his homily with words from St. Faustina's *Diary*: "I feel certain that my mission will not come to an end upon my death, but will begin."[225] This is exactly what Jesus had called for through His servant Faustina.

Canonization

As with a beautification, before anyone can be canonized by the Catholic Church, a thorough process of investigation is carried out. In addition, an indisputable miracle (a second one) needs to occur due to the intercession of the beatified person.

On April 30, 2000, before 250,000 pilgrims and television cameras going out to the world, Pope John Paul II canonized Blessed Maria Faustina Kowalska in Rome on Divine Mercy Sunday, during the Great Jubilee Year 2000. During his canonization homily, Pope John Paul II said, "The Second Sunday of Easter from now on throughout the Church will be called 'Divine Mercy Sunday.'"[226]

He also stated, "By this act of canonization of Saint Faustina I intend today to pass this message on to the third millennium. I pass it on to all people, so that they will learn to know ever better the true face of God and the true face of their neighbour. In fact, love of God and love of one's neighbour are inseparable."

The Divine Mercy pope ended his homily with, "And you, St. Faustina, a gift of God to our time, a gift from the land of Poland to the whole Church, obtain for us an awareness of the depth of Divine Mercy; help us to have a living experience of it and to bear witness to it among our brothers and sisters. May your message of light and hope spread throughout the world, spurring sinners to conversion, calming rivalries and hatred, and opening individuals and nations to the practice of brotherhood."[227]

Afterwards, during a banquet celebration, St. John Paul II shared that canonizing St. Faustina was the happiest day of his life!

Jesus' deep desire

Jesus often impressed upon His Secretary of Divine Mercy the importance of calling upon His Mercy and of trusting Him. Many times, Jesus spoke to Faustina about hardened sinners and how His Sacred Heart desires that they call out to Him so that He can impart His great Mercy to them. One of these times, He said:

> [Let] the greatest sinners place their trust in My mercy. They have the right before others to trust in the abyss of My mercy. My daughter, write about My mercy towards tormented souls. Souls that make an appeal to My mercy delight Me. To such

souls I grant even more graces than they ask. I cannot punish even the greatest sinner if he makes an appeal to My compassion, but on the contrary, I justify him in My unfathomable and inscrutable mercy. Write: before I come as a just Judge, I first open wide the door of My mercy. He who refuses to pass through the door of My mercy must pass through the door of My justice..."[228]

We see how important it is to Jesus that all souls be saved. He desires to grant abundant graces to even the most hardened sinners! However, they must repent and trust in His Love and Mercy for them.

During a long conversation our friend Faustina had with Our Lord, He told her:

How very much I desire the salvation of souls! My dearest secretary, write that I want to pour out My divine life into human souls and sanctify them, if only they were willing to accept My grace. The greatest sinners would achieve great sanctity, if only they would trust in My mercy. The very inner depths of My being are filled to overflowing with mercy, and it is being poured out upon all I have created. My delight is to act in a human soul and to fill it with My mercy and to justify it. My kingdom on earth is My life in the human soul. Write, My secretary, that I Myself am the spiritual guide of souls — and I guide them indirectly through the priest, and lead each one to sanctity by a road known to Me alone.[229]

Saint Faustina's mission

Jesus told His Secretary of Divine Mercy, "I sent prophets wielding thunderbolts to My people. Today I am sending you with My mercy to the people of the whole world. I do not want to punish aching mankind, but I desire to heal it, pressing it to My Merciful Heart."[230]

Jesus also told St. Faustina, **"My child you are My delight, you are the comfort of My Heart. I grant you as many graces as you can hold. As often as you want to make Me happy, speak to the world about My great and unfathomable mercy."**[231] Our Lord also calls us to be His delight and tell the world about His great love and Mercy. Let's pray for the graces to do so.

Saint Faustina's mission is encapsulated in these three tasks:

1. To highlight, clarify, and proclaim to the world the truth revealed in the Holy Scriptures about the merciful love of God for every human being.

2. To entreat God's mercy for the whole world, especially through new forms of devotion to The Divine Mercy given by the Lord Jesus. These are: The Image of The Divine Mercy with the inscription: "Jesus, I trust in You"; the Feast of the Divine Mercy on the Second Sunday of Easter, (Divine Mercy Sunday); The Divine Mercy Chaplet; and the prayer and meditation on His Passion at the Hour of Great Mercy (3 o'clock in the afternoon).

3. To inspire the apostolic movement of the Divine Mercy, which continues St. Faustina's mission of proclaiming and entreating God's mercy for the world, as well as striving for perfection in the footsteps of St. Faustina. It consists in showing child-like trust in God, in desiring to do His will, and in the attitude of mercy toward one's neighbor.[232]

Sister Faustina desired with all her heart to lovingly do everything Our Lord wanted her to do and to love Him beyond measure. She once told her beloved Jesus, "My Jesus, You know that from my earliest years I have wanted to become a great saint; that is to say, I have wanted to love You with a love so great that there would be no soul who has hitherto loved You so."[233] Her humble loving words stir our own hearts to lovingly strive for holiness and to do God's holy will.

It's important to note here that because of Saint Faustina's obedience to God's holy will in carrying out the mission of the Divine Mercy, her charism also yielded the Apostolic Movement of the Divine Mercy to proclaim the message of Mercy to the world through the testimony of life, deeds, words and prayer. Jesus revealed the idea of this Movement in Vilnius in 1935 when Jesus ordered her to set up a new Congregation "which will proclaim the mercy of God to the world and, by its prayers, obtain it for the world."[234] Jesus told her, "**I desire that there be such a Congregation.**"[235] Even after the humble Saint's death, Divine Mercy was being proclaimed in many ways including through the new Congregation of The Sisters of Our Lady of Mercy.

Saint Faustina works hard even after her death

Saint Faustina was certainly in good company when she surmised, "I feel certain that my mission will not come to an end upon my death, but will begin." Other saints were gifted to know and express the same. Saint Faustina further expressed, "O doubting souls, I will draw aside for you the veils of heaven to convince you of God's goodness, so that you will no longer continue to wound with your distrust the sweetest Heart of Jesus. God is Love and Mercy."[236]

As we know, our humble friend was not just concerned for her own salvation. After all, she was to tell the world of God's great Love and Mercy so that they could get to Heaven one day too. Faustina expressed, "Poor earth, I will not forget you. Although I feel that I will be immediately drowned in God as in an ocean of happiness, that will not be an obstacle to my returning to earth to encourage souls and incite them to trust in God's mercy. Indeed, this immersion in God will give me the possibility of boundless action."[237]

After she penned these words in her *Diary,* she heard Satan causing a noisy commotion in her cell. She further wrote, "As I write this, I hear Satan grinding his teeth. He cannot stand God's mercy, and keeps banging things in my cell. But I feel so much of

God's power within me that it does not even bother me that the enemy of our salvation gets angry, and I quietly keep on writing."[238]

Another gift of Saint Faustina to us is that she is a dispenser of grace! We can seek her intercession, asking for graces, according to God's holy will. After all, Jesus told her, **"Do whatever you wish, distribute graces as you will, to whom you will and when you will."**[239] Don't forget to ask her for graces!

What is our part?

What is our part in this journey of Divine Mercy? We must be certain — our response to Jesus' Divine Mercy is not once a year on Divine Mercy Sunday. Jesus, specifically asked Sr. Faustina to spread the message of Divine Mercy and that we should always be merciful to others. Not only should we trust in God's Mercy for our own souls, we must pray for all souls! Jesus demands this of us — to pray earnestly to save souls — our families, neighbors, the dying (we can also bring the Divine Mercy Image to them, when possible), the Holy Souls in Purgatory, and for sinners. A big part of St. Faustina's mission was to pray for the dying and the Holy Souls in Purgatory. We can follow her example.

Hopefully, through reading this book and becoming more enlightened about Jesus' Divine Mercy through the life of the humble mystic St. Faustina, you will have a greater desire to live the Divine Mercy message and to impart it to others.

Divine Mercy is mankind's last hope of salvation. Jesus said: **"Souls who spread the honor of My mercy I shield through their entire lives as a tender mother her infant, and at the hour of death I will not be a Judge for them, but the Merciful Savior. At that last hour, a soul has nothing with which to defend itself except My mercy. Happy is the soul that during its lifetime immersed itself in the Fountain of Mercy, because justice will have no hold on it."**[240]

I'll leave you with another bit of wisdom from our friend Faustina. She wrote, "He gave me to understand how fleeting all earthly things are, and [how] everything that appears great disappears like smoke, and does not give the soul freedom, but weariness. Happy the soul that understands these things and with only one foot touches the earth."[241]

Let us strive to become detached from fleeting earthly things and like Faustina, only one foot touching the earth to work out our salvation. Let us spread the honor of Jesus' Divine Mercy and also have recourse to our dear friend St. Faustina, who can pray for great graces for us.

JESUS, I TRUST IN YOU!

 ## Something to Think About

You've reached the end of my telling of the life of St. Maria Faustina Kowalska of the Most Blessed Sacrament! Don't forget to read the prayer Appendix and also my message to you in the Afterword.

Take a few moments to quietly and prayerfully ponder and savor what you have learned in this last chapter. There is much to think about and take to your heart! Ask St. Faustina to accompany you in prayer.

 ## Pray

Dear Jesus and Mary, please guide me. Jesus, I trust in You! Dear St. Faustina, please grant many graces to me, pray for me, and assist me in living a holy merciful life.

 ## A Merciful Action

Strive to show others the importance of detaching from fleeting things and focus on salvation. Do all you can to help others to Heaven! Be a radiant holy spark!

Afterword

I have thought of you and prayed for you as I wrote this book. Every book I write is a special journey for me. I thoroughly enjoyed writing about our friend St. Faustina and getting even closer to her and her writings in order to help others get to know her and to learn of the message of Divine Mercy.

We certainly don't have to dust off history pages to learn about our friend St. Faustina, for she is not some old fashioned person we'd have trouble getting know. After all, she walked the Earth during the twentieth century. She was down to earth, had a pleasant and glowing demeanor and had quite a sense of humor, too.

Interestingly, I sat down to do the actual writing of this book on October 5, 2022, which is St. Faustina's feast day and the anniversary of her death. Prior to that date, I had started to plan the writing and had mapped out the chapters, had written a bit, and had also spoken to an illustrator about what I would need. I knew how I wanted to start the book and planned to open with something very intriguing in St. Faustina's life to draw the reader in and then I would usher them back to the very beginning to tell her whole story. In fact, I had already started writing the first chapter.

However, on the morning of October 5, it seemed that the Heavens had opened wide. Rain poured down in sheets! Immediately, I knew without a doubt how I had to change my original plan and instead, begin the book with the miracle of the beggar at the gate. On that miraculous day, the Heavens also opened wide with pouring torrential rain. As you read in the first chapter, St. Faustina encountered Jesus Himself at the gate.

And, so, I began my labor of love for you.

I'll also share something with you that you might enjoy and find interesting. It occurred during the writing of this book. When I was getting closer to finishing the book, the entire manuscript, without prior warning suddenly disappeared! Even though I was writing on a brand-new computer, I encountered this frightening loss. I searched and searched and my computer put out scary notices telling me the document did not exist.

Even with saving my work constantly, the manuscript had somehow disappeared! This was months of hard work. All the while, I trusted God would help me — somehow — that no matter what, all would be well — eventually. I also knew that might mean I had to write it all over again!

You might now recall the fact that the evil one hates Divine Mercy. The more I searched, the more complicated it became. I decided to quickly call a computer technician. I knew from past experience that I had to be very careful. I needed immediate help because if I did the wrong thing, I could lose the entire manuscript for good. I dialed the phone number, hoping and praying for someone who would understand my dilemma and be able to help me. *Please God!* I prayed.

"Hello my name is Angel. May I ask your name?"

You can probably imagine my surprise and delight to be speaking with someone named Angel! God is pretty amazing like that! Angel was a true Godsend! We had the most amazing conversation. He ended up telling me that he had served in the military for a number of years and that he always counts his blessings and continues to put his "life into the hand of the MAN above." That really told me something about him.

Well, it took almost two hours to fix the problem and thank God my manuscript was saved. The last few minutes (or more!), we shared with one another about our Faith in God and even about writing. You see, this man has a book in him, just waiting to be written. I believe God put me in Angel's life to encourage him to write the book that has been on his heart for years now. And God certainly put him into my life to inspire Faith in my own heart (not to mention the fact that Angel had saved my book)!

I told Angel that I was so delighted when I heard him tell me his name at the beginning of what would be a truly blessed conversation — one I won't forget.

Later that evening, I literally stopped in my tracks. It suddenly dawned on me that I had been working on the chapter about ANGELS (and demons) when my manuscript disappeared and all of the above happened! I hadn't thought about that when I was in the midst of frantically (and prayerfully!) trying to save my book. Pretty amazing!

Finally, I hope you have gotten to know St. Faustina and might consider her as a very special friend. I consider her not only a friend, but a dear sister. Call upon her. Ask for her help. Please endeavor to strive very hard to trust God with your life. Ask Jesus to grant graces to you for this reason. Ask St. Faustina for graces! In addition, I hope you'll be able to carve out time to read the *Diary* in full.

Finally, I encourage you to pray, and with God's grace, to allow your holy spark to burst into a "fire of mercy" for the world! God bless you! God love you!

Yours in Jesus, Mary, and Joseph,
Donna-Marie Cooper O'Boyle
Feast of the Epiphany, January 6, 2023

Appendix of Prayers

The Litany of Loreto
(Prayed by the Kowalska family)

Lord have mercy.
Christ have mercy.
Lord have mercy.
Christ hear us.
Christ graciously hear us.

God, the Father of heaven, **have mercy on us.**

God the Son, Redeemer of the world,
God the Holy Spirit,
Holy Trinity, one God,

Holy Mary, **pray for us.**
Holy Mother of God,
Holy Virgin of virgins,
Mother of Christ,
Mother of the Church,
Mother of Mercy,
Mother of divine grace,
Mother of Hope,
Mother most pure,
Mother most chaste,
Mother inviolate,
Mother undefiled,
Mother most amiable,
Mother admirable,
Mother of good counsel,
Mother of our Creator,

Mother of our Saviour,
Virgin most prudent,
Virgin most venerable,
Virgin most renowned,
Virgin most powerful,
Virgin most merciful,
Virgin most faithful,
Mirror of justice,
Seat of wisdom,
Cause of our joy,
Spiritual vessel,
Vessel of honour,
Singular vessel of devotion,
Mystical rose,
Tower of David,
Tower if ivory,
House of gold,
Ark of the covenant,
Gate of heaven,
Morning star,
Health of the sick,
Refuge of sinners,
Solace of Migrants,
Comfort of the afflicted,
Help of Christians,
Queen of Angels,
Queen of Patriarchs,
Queen of Prophets,
Queen of Apostles,
Queen of Martyrs,
Queen of Confessors,
Queen of Virgins,
Queen of all Saints,
Queen conceived without original sin,
Queen assumed into heaven,
Queen of the most holy Rosary,

Queen of families,
Queen of peace.

Lamb of God, who takes away the sins of the world,
spare us, O Lord.

Lamb of God, who takes away the sins of the world,
graciously hear us, O Lord.

Lamb of God, who takes away the sins of the world,
have mercy on us.

Pray for us, O holy Mother of God.
That we may be made worthy of the promises of Christ.

Let us pray.

Grant, we beseech thee,
O Lord God,
that we, your servants,
may enjoy perpetual health of mind and body;
and by the glorious intercession of the Blessed Mary, ever Virgin,
may be delivered from present sorrow,
and obtain eternal joy.
Through Christ our Lord.
Amen.

Saint Faustina's Simple Act of Trust

"Do what You will with me, O Jesus;
I will adore You in everything. May Your will be
done in me, O my Lord and my God,
and I will praise Your infinite mercy."

— *Diary*, 78

Divine Mercy Chaplet

The Chaplet of Mercy is recited using ordinary Rosary beads of five decades. At the National Shrine of The Divine Mercy in Stockbridge, Massachusetts, the Chaplet is preceded by two opening prayers from the Diary of Saint Maria Faustina Kowalska and followed by a closing prayer.

How to Pray the Chaplet of Divine Mercy

1. Make the Sign of the Cross.

2. Say the optional Opening Prayer.

3. Say the "Our Father."

4. Say the "Hail Mary."

5. Say the Apostles' Creed.

6. Say the "Eternal Father."

7. Say 10 "For the sake of His sorrowful Passion" on the "Hail Mary" beads.

8. Repeat for four more decades, saying "Eternal Father" on the "Our Father" bead and then 10 "For the Sake of His sorrowful Passion" on the following "Hail Mary" beads.

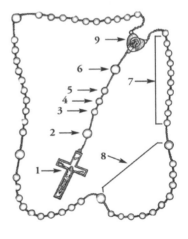

9. At the conclusion of the five decades, on the medallion say the "Holy God," the concluding doxology, three times.

10. Say the optional Closing Prayer.

Prayers of the Chaplet of Divine Mercy

1. The Sign of the Cross: In the name of the Father, and of the Son, and of the Holy Spirit. Amen.

2. Opening Prayers *(optional)*: You expired, Jesus, but the source of life gushed forth for souls, and the ocean of mercy opened up for the whole world. O Fount of Life, unfathomable Divine Mercy, envelop the whole world and empty Yourself out upon us (*Diary*, 1319).

O Blood and Water, which gushed forth from the Heart of Jesus as a fount of mercy for us, I trust in You! *(three times)* (84).

3. The Our Father: Our Father, who art in heaven, hallowed be Thy name; Thy kingdom come; Thy will be done on earth as it is in heaven. Give us this day our daily bread; and forgive us our trespasses as we forgive those who trespass against us; and lead us not into temptation, but deliver us from evil. Amen.

4. The Hail Mary: Hail Mary, full of grace. The Lord is with thee. Blessed art thou among women, and blessed is the fruit of thy womb, Jesus. Holy Mary, Mother of God, pray for us sinners, now and at the hour of our death. Amen.

5. The Apostles' Creed: I believe in God, the Father almighty, Creator of heaven and earth, and in Jesus Christ, his only Son, our Lord, who was conceived by the Holy Spirit, born of the Virgin Mary, suffered under Pontius Pilate, was crucified, died, and was buried; he descended into hell; on the third day he rose again from the dead; he ascended into heaven, and is seated at the right hand of God the Father almighty; from there he will come to judge the living and the dead. I believe in the Holy Spirit, the Holy Catholic Church, the communion of saints, the forgiveness of sins, the resurrection of the body, and life ever-lasting. Amen.

6. On the "Our Father" *bead before each decade:* Eternal Father, I offer You the Body and Blood, Soul and Divinity of Your dearly beloved Son, Our Lord Jesus Christ, in atonement for our sins and those of the whole world (476).

7. On the "Hail Mary" *beads of each decade:* For the sake of His sorrowful Passion, have mercy on us and on the whole world.

8. Repeat "Eternal Father" and **"For the Sake of His sorrowful Passion"** *(Numbers 6 & 7)* Prayers for four more decades.

9. After 5 decades, the concluding doxology *(three times)*: Holy God, Holy Mighty One, Holy Immortal One, have mercy on us and on the whole world.

10. Closing Prayer *(optional)*: Eternal God, in whom mercy is endless and the treasury of compassion inexhaustible, look kindly upon us and increase Your mercy in us, that in difficult moments we might not despair nor become despondent, but with great confidence submit ourselves to Your holy will, which is Love and Mercy Itself (950). Amen.

The wording of the Apostles' Creed conforms with the *Roman Missal*.

The Chaplet of Mercy as a Novena

In addition to the Novena to Divine Mercy (see *Diary*, 1209-1229), which our Lord gave to St. Maria Faustina for her own personal use, He revealed to her a powerful prayer that He wanted everyone to say — the Chaplet of Mercy. Saint Faustina prayed the chaplet almost constantly, especially for the dying, and the Lord urged her to encourage others to say it, too, promising extraordinary graces to those who recited this special prayer.

The chaplet can be said anytime, but the Lord specifically asked that it be recited as a novena, especially on the nine days before the Feast of Mercy. And He promised, **"By this novena [of Chaplets], I will grant every possible grace to souls."** (796)

We can pray this Novena of Chaplets for our own personal intentions, or we can offer it together with the Novena to Divine Mercy for the daily intentions dictated by our Lord to St. Faustina.

A Prayer For Divine Mercy

O Greatly Merciful God, Infinite Goodness, today all mankind calls out from the abyss of its misery to Your mercy — to Your compassion, O God; and it is with its mighty voice of misery that it cries out. Gracious God, do not reject the prayer of this earth's exiles! O Lord, Goodness beyond our understanding, Who are acquainted with our misery through and through, and know that by our own power we cannot ascend to You, we implore You: anticipate us with Your grace and keep on increasing Your mercy in us, that we may faithfully do Your holy will all through our life and at death's hour. Let the omnipotence of Your mercy shield us from the darts of our salvation's enemies, that we may with confidence, as Your children, await Your [Son's] final coming — that day known to You alone. And we expect to obtain everything promised us by Jesus in spite of all our wretchedness. For Jesus is our Hope: Through His merciful Heart as through an open gate, we pass through to heaven (*Diary*, 1570). Amen.

Blood and Water Prayer

Jesus told St. Faustina: **"Call upon My mercy on behalf of sinners; I desire their salvation. When you say this prayer, with a contrite heart and with faith on behalf of some sinner, I will give him the grace of conversion. This is the prayer:**

'O Blood and Water, which gushed forth from the Heart of Jesus as a fount of Mercy for us, I trust in You.'" (186-187)

Acknowledgments

I am deeply grateful to my parents, Eugene Joseph and Alexandra Mary Cooper, for bringing me into the world and raising me in a large Catholic family. To my brothers and sisters — Alice Jean, Gene, Gary, Barbara, Tim, Michael, and David — thank you for being a wonderful part of my life.

My heartfelt gratitude goes to my husband, Dave, and my beloved children — Justin, Chaldea, Jessica, Joseph, and Mary-Catherine — for their continued love and support, and to my precious grandsons, Shepherd and Leo. I love you all dearly!

Special thanks to my friend, Servant of God Fr. John Hardon, SJ, who spiritually directed and encouraged me, and is no doubt continuing from Heaven! Also, an exuberant thank you to dear Mother Teresa for playing a huge role in shaping me spiritually and for being a mother to me, which I know she continues even now.

I owe special thanks to Marian Press for asking that I write this book, to the Very Rev. Chris Alar, MIC, publisher of Marian Press; to Dr. Robert Stackpole, for thoroughly proofing for theological accuracy; and to Dr. Joe McAleer, Chris Sparks, Mary Clark, Tad Floridis, and the wonderful team at Marian Press who helped get this book out to you!

I thank my dear "Sisters in Christ: United Under Mary's Mantle" for their generous prayers for the ministry.

And thank you to Michael Ornido, whose illustrations bring St. Faustina's incredible journey more alive to the reader.

Finally, I am extremely thankful for my readership, viewership, and listenership, and to all those I meet in my travels. Thank you for being part of my fascinating journey through life! I pray for you. Please pray for me, too. God bless you!

About the Author

Donna-Marie Cooper O'Boyle loves to share stories to inspire faith in others. She is a TV host, an international speaker, a pilgrimage and retreat leader, an authority on the life of St. Maria Faustina Kowalska, and an award-winning and best-selling author and journalist. She enjoyed a decade-long friendship with St. Mother Teresa of Calcutta and became a lay Missionary of Charity. For many years, her spiritual director was Servant of God John A. Hardon, SJ, who also served as one of Mother Teresa's spiritual directors.

Donna-Marie is the EWTN television host of *Everyday Blessings for Catholic Moms, Catholic Mom's Cafe,* and *Feeding Your Family's Soul.* She was invited by the Holy See in 2008 to participate in an international congress for women at the Vatican to mark the 20th anniversary of the apostolic letter *Mulieris Dignitatem (On the Dignity and Vocation of Women).*

Donna-Marie's more than 35 books on faith and family include *52 Weeks with Saint Faustina: A Year of Grace and Mercy* (Marian Press); *Christmas Joy with Grandma!* (Marian Press); *Family Consecration to Jesus Through Mary;* and her memoir, *The Kiss of Jesus.* She is a contributor and General Editor of the *Divine Mercy Catholic Bible.* Her work has been featured in many Catholic magazines, national newspapers, and online media platforms. Donna-Marie has received awards from organizations such as the Catholic Press Association, The National Federation of Press Women, The Military Council of Catholic Women, and the American Cancer Society.

Perhaps most importantly, Donna-Marie is a Catholic wife, mother, grandmother, and friend.

Visit **www.donnacooperoboyle.com**

Notes

1 *Diary of St. Faustina Kowalska: Divine Mercy in My Soul* (Stockbridge, MA: Marian Press, 1987), n. 1312.

2 Ibid., n. 1313.

3 Ibid., n. 1732.

4 Pope John Paul II, Homily, Canonization of Saint Faustina, April 30, 2000, 2. www.vatican.va/content/john-paul-ii/en/homilies/2000/documents/hf_jp-ii_hom_20000430_faustina.html

5 Grzegorz Gorny and Janusz Rosikon, *Trust: In Saint Faustina's Footsteps* (San Francisco, CA: Ignatius Press, 2014), 33.

6 *Diary of St. Faustina Kowalska*, n. 1404.

7 Gorny and Rosikin, *Trust: In Saint Faustina's Footsteps,* 39.

8 *Diary of St. Faustina Kowalska*, n. 7.

9 Ibid., n. 8.

10 Ewa K. Czaczkowska, *Faustina: the mystic and her message* (Stockbridge, MA: Marian Press, 2014), 68.

11 Ibid., n. 9.

12 Ibid.

13 Ibid.

14 Ibid., n. 10.

15 Czaczkowska, 69.

16 *Diary of St. Faustina Kowalska*, n. 11.

17 Ibid.

18 Ibid., n. 12.

19 Ibid., n. 13.

20 Ibid., n. 15.

21 Ibid., n. 16.

22 Ibid., n. 13.

23 Ibid., n. 13.

24 Czaczkowska, 85.

25 Czaczkowska, 85.

26 *Diary of St. Faustina Kowalska*, n. 14.

27 Gorny and Rosikin, *Trust: In Saint Faustina's Footsteps,* 60.

28 *Diary of St. Faustina Kowalska*, n. 17.

29 Sister Sophia Michalenko, CMGT, *The Life of Faustina Kowalska: An Authorized Biography* (Cincinnati, OH: Servant Books, 1999) 30.

30 *Diary of St. Faustina Kowalska*, n. 18.

31 Ibid., n. 19.

32 Ibid., n. 20.

33 Ibid.

34 Ibid., n. 29.

35 Ibid., n. 165.

36 Ibid., n. 166.

37 Ibid., n. 151.

[38] Ibid.
[39] Ibid., n. 21.
[40] Michalenko, *The Life of Faustina Kowalska*, 32.
[41] *Diary of St. Faustina Kowalska*, n. 22.
[42] Ibid.
[43] Gorny and Rosikin, *Trust: In Saint Faustina's Footsteps*, 77.
[44] *Diary of St. Faustina Kowalska*, n. 23.
[45] Ibid., n. 101.
[46] Ibid., n. 23.
[47] Ibid., n. 27.
[48] Gorny and Rosikin, *Trust: In Saint Faustina's Footsteps*, 86.
[49] *Diary of St. Faustina Kowalska*, n. 27.
[50] Ibid., n. 150.
[51] Ibid., n. 47.
[52] Ibid., n. 48.
[53] Ibid., n. 49.
[54] Ibid., n. 50.
[55] Ibid., n. 51.
[56] Ibid., n. 52.
[57] Ibid.
[58] Ibid., n. 53.
[59] Ibid., n. 55.
[60] Ibid.
[61] Ibid., n. 635.
[62] Ibid., n. 11.
[63] Ibid.
[64] Ibid., n. 240.
[65] Ibid.
[66] Ibid., n. 608.
[67] Ibid., n. 609.
[68] Ibid., n. 1731.
[69] Ibid., n. 25.
[70] Ibid., n. 325.
[71] Ibid., n. 330.
[72] Ibid., n. 449.
[73] Ibid., n. 1746.
[74] Ibid., n. 1437.
[75] Ibid., n. 246.
[76] Ibid., n. 314.
[77] Ibid., n. 709.
[78] Ibid., n. 412.
[79] Ibid., n. 40.
[80] Ibid., n. 843.
[81] Ibid., n. 240.
[82] Ibid., n. 20.
[83] Ibid., n. 21.
[84] Ibid., n. 58.
[85] Ibid.

[86] Ibid., n. 1382.

[87] Ibid., n. 1723.

[88] Ibid., n. 835.

[89] Ibid., n. 594.

[90] Ibid., n. 1185, 1186, 1187.

[91] Ibid., n. 1738.

[92] Ibid., n. 36.

[93] Ibid.

[94] Ibid., n. 1209

[95] Ibid., n. 1226

[96] Ibid., n. 314

[97] Ibid., n. 1724

[98] Ibid., n. 1111.

[99] *Diary of St. Faustina Kowalska,* n. 630.

[100] Donna-Marie Cooper O'Boyle, *52 Weeks with Saint Faustina: A Year of Grace and Mercy* (Stockbridge, MA: Marian Press, 2018), 266.

[101] *Diary of St. Faustina Kowalska,* n. 471

[102] Ibid., n. 630.

[103] Ibid., n. 412.

[104] Ibid., n. 419.

[105] Ibid., n. 820.

[106] Ibid., n. 828.

[107] Cooper O'Boyle, *52 Weeks with Saint Faustina,* 268.

[108] *Diary of St. Faustina Kowalska,* n. 1676.

[109] Ibid., xlii.

[110] Ibid., n. 1287.

[111] Ibid., n. 1405.

[112] Ibid., n. 1465.

[113] Ibid., n. 741.

[114] Ibid., n. 1145.

[115] Ibid., n. 150.

[116] Ibid., n. 529.

[117] Ibid., n. 1578.

[118] Ibid., n. 1074.

[119] Ibid., n. 1599.

[120] Ibid., n. 65.

[121] Ibid.

[122] Ibid., n. 66.

[123] Ibid., n. 6.

[124] Ibid., n. 1693.

[125] Ibid., n. 1074.

[126] Ibid., n. 839.

[127] Fr. Michael Sopoćko, *Before She Was a Saint, She Was a Secretary,* www.thedivinemercy.org/articles/she-was-saint-she-was-secretary.

[128] Ibid., n. 270.

[129] Ibid., n. 1471.

[130] Cooper O'Boyle, *52 Weeks with Saint Faustina,* 289.

[131] Pope John Paul II, *The Many Streams of the Spirituality of St. Faustina,*

www.thedivinemercy.org/articles/many-streams-spirituality-st-faustina.

132 *L'Osservatore Romano*, Weekly Edition in English, 3 May 2000, page 2, *St Faustina, Apostle of Divine Mercy,* [https://www.ewtn.com/catholicism/library/st-faustina-apostle-of-divine-mercy-5458]

133 See the Sisters of Our Lady of Mercy website: www.sisterfaustina.org

134 *Diary of St. Faustina Kowalska,* n. 429.

135 Ibid., n. 786.

136 Ibid.

137 Czaczkowska, 301.

138 *Diary of St. Faustina Kowalska,* n. 561.

139 Ibid., n. 369.

140 Ibid., n. 267.

141 Ibid., n. 737.

142 Saint Teresa of Calcutta in a personal letter (February 18, 1988) to the author of this book.

143 Saint Teresa of Calcutta in a personal letter (August 28, 1993) to the author of this book.

144 *Diary of St. Faustina Kowalska,* n. 65.

145 *Diary of St. Faustina Kowalska,* n. 948.

146 Ibid., n. 1372.

147 Ibid., n. 332.

148 Ibid., n. 56.

149 Ibid.

150 Ibid., n. 1092.

151 Ibid.

152 Ibid., n. 270.

153 Ibid., n. 267.

154 Ibid., n. 1415.

155 Cooper-O'Boyle, *52 Weeks with Saint Faustina,* 115.

156 *Diary of St. Faustina Kowalska,* n. 593.

157 Ibid., n. 1779.

158 Ibid., n. 246.

159 *Diary of St. Faustina Kowalska,* n. 817.

160 Ibid., n. 1602.

161 Ibid., n. 1448.

162 Ibid., n. 1602.

163 "Exorcist says sacraments are more powerful than rite of exorcism," *Catholic Canada*: https://catholicanada.com/2021/11/exorcist-says-sacraments-are-more-powerful-than-rite-of-exorcism-the-most-powerful-thing-the-church-offers-to-cast-out-demons-is-the-confessional/

164 Pope John Paul II, *Ecclesia de Eucharistia* (April 17, 2003), 9. www.vatican.va/content/john-paul-ii/en/encyclicals/documents/hf_jp-ii_enc_20030417_eccl-de-euch.html

165 *Diary of St. Faustina Kowalska,* n. 1392.

166 Ibid., n. 1826.

167 Ibid., n. 1392.

168 Ibid., n. 1804.

169 Ibid., n. 1806.

[170] Ibid., n. 1821.

[171] Ibid., n. 1811.

[172] Ibid., n. 1385.

[173] Ibid., n. 1094.

[174] Ibid., n. 582.

[175] Ibid., n. 622.

[176] Ibid., n. 1107.

[177] Cooper O'Boyle, *52 Weeks with Saint Faustina*, 00

[178] Ibid., n. 1810.

[179] Ibid., n. 1578.

[180] Ibid., n. 1760.

[181] Ibid., n. 1127.

[182] Ibid., n. 147.

[183] Ibid., n. 872.

[184] Ibid., n. 860.

[185] Ibid., n. 268.

[186] Ibid., n. 1588-1589.

[187] Ibid., n. 811.

[188] Ibid., n. 186-187.

[189] Ibid., n. 1601.

[190] Ibid., n. 718.

[191] Ibid., n. 367.

[192] Ibid., n. 1184.

[193] Ibid., n. 1779.

[194] Ibid.

[195] John Paul II, "Dedication of the Shrine of Divine Mercy: Homily of the Holy Father John Paul II," 17 Aug 2002 www.vatican.va/content/john-paul-ii/en/homilies/2002/documents/hf_jp-ii_hom_20020817_shrine-divine-mercy.html

[196] Cited in Maria Tarnowska, *Saint Sister Faustina: Her Life and Mission* (London: Veritas, fourth edition, 2000), 201.

[197] See "Saint Faustina the Theologian," *The Divine Mercy* October 12, 2017: www.thedivinemercy.org/articles/saint-faustina-theologian

[198] *Diary of St. Faustina Kowalska*, n. 300, 301.

[199] Ibid., n. 1577.

[200] Ibid., n. 635.

[201] Ibid., n. 47.

[202] Ibid., n. 313.

[203] Ibid., n. 48.

[204] Ibid., n. 326.

[205] Ibid., n. 299.

[206] Ibid., n. 1190.

[207] Ibid., n. 699.

[208] Ibid., n. 1379.

[209] Ibid., n. 1732.

[210] Ibid., n. 796.

[211] Ibid., n. 474.

[212] Ibid., n. 476.

213 Ibid., n. 810.

214 Ibid., n. 811.

215 Ibid., n. 1572.

216 Ibid., n. 1209.

217 Ibid., n. 163.

218 Ibid., n. 742.

219 Ibid.

220 See Pope John Paul II, homily, Consecration of the Shrine of Divine Mercy, Kraków-Łagiewniki, Poland (August 17, 2002): https://www.thedivinemercy.org/message/john-paul-ii/homilies/1981-11-22

221 See Pope John Paul II, homily, Beatification of St. Faustina (August 17, 2002): The Divine Mercy, [https://www.thedivinemercy.org/message/john-paul-ii/homilies/1993-04-1] From: L'Osservatore Romano, April 21, 1993

222 Pope John Paul II, *Consecration of the Shrine of Divine Mercy.*

223 See EWTN, "The Process of Beatification and Canonization": www.ewtn.com/catholicism/library/process-of-beatification-and-canonization-13747

224 Ibid.

225 *Diary of St. Maria Faustina Kowalska,* n. 281.

226 Pope John Paul II, Homily for the Canonization of Sr. Mary Faustina Kowalska, Apr. 30, 2000, 4. www.vatican.va/content/john-paul-ii/en/homilies/2000/documents/hf_jp-ii_hom_20000430_faustina.html.

227 Ibid., n. 8.

228 *Diary of St. Faustina Kowalska,* n. 1146.

229 Ibid., n. 1784.

230 Ibid., n. 1588.

231 Ibid., n. 164.

232 Ibid., xx-xxi.

233 Ibid., n. 1372.

234 Ibid., n. 436

235 Ibid., n. 437

236 Ibid., n. 281.

237 Ibid., n. 1582.

238 Ibid., n. 1583.

239 Ibid., n. 31.

240 Ibid., n. 1075.

241 Ibid., n. 1141.

More from Donna-Marie Cooper O'Boyle

Christmas Joy with Grandma!

Take an Advent journey with Joseph, Anne-Marie, and Grandmother! Together, you'll discover the story of Christmas and get ready to welcome Jesus into your own heart and home.

Beautifully illustrated, this gentle, loving introduction to the true meaning of Christmas by Donna-Marie Cooper O'Boyle will become a beloved book for every family and revisited each holiday season. Paperback. 48 pages. Y110-CHSB

52 Weeks with Saint Faustina:
A Year of Grace and Mercy

Spend a year with St. Faustina! Perfect to begin any time of the year, this collection of weekly meditations and activities by Donna-Marie Cooper O'Boyle, author of *The Domestic Church: Room by Room*, guides readers on a 52-week spiritual pilgrimage through the life and teachings of the Secretary and Apostle of Divine Mercy, St. Faustina Kowalska (1905-1938). Paperback. 390 pages. Y110-WEEKS

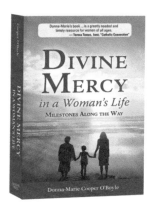

Divine Mercy in a Woman's Life:
Milestones Along the Way

What does it mean for a woman to live according to Divine Mercy spirituality? In this loving look at life as lived by faithful female Catholics, Donna-Marie Cooper O'Boyle has given modern women an important guide to letting the rays of Divine Mercy touch them, transform them, and flow through them to the world. Paperback. 416 pages. Y110-DMFW

Call 1-800-462-7426 or ShopMercy.org

Essential Divine Mercy Resources

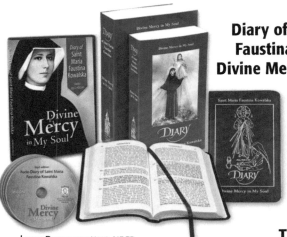

Diary of Saint Maria Faustina Kowalska: Divine Mercy in My Soul

LARGE PAPERBACK: Y110-NBFD
COMPACT PAPERBACK: Y110-DNBF
DELUXE LEATHER-BOUND EDITION: Y110-DDBURG
AUDIO DIARY MP3 EDITION: Y110-ADMP3

The Divine Mercy Message and Devotion
Fr. Seraphim Michalenko, MIC, with
Vinny Flynn and Robert A. Stackpole
Y110-M17

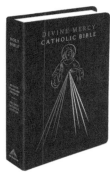

Divine Mercy Catholic Bible

Many Catholics ask what version of the Bible is best to read. In the Revised Standard Version Catholic Edition (RSV-CE) you have the answer.

The *Divine Mercy Catholic Bible* clearly shows the astounding revelation of Divine Mercy amidst the timeless truths of Sacred Scripture. This Bible includes 175 Mercy Moments and 19 articles that explain how God encounters us with mercy through His Word and Sacraments. Y110-BIDM

Explaining the Faith Series
Understanding Divine Mercy
Fr. Chris Alar, MIC

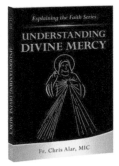

The entire Divine Mercy message and devotion is summarized in one, easy-to-read book! Explaining the teaching of Jesus Christ as given to St. Faustina, *Understanding Divine Mercy* by Fr. Chris Alar, MIC, has it all. Written in his highly conversational and energetic style, this first book in his *Explaining the Faith* series will deepen your love for God and help you understand why Jesus called Divine Mercy "mankind's last hope of salvation." Paperback. 184 pages. Y110-EFBK

Call 1-800-462-7426 or ShopMercy.org

Enriching Reading for the Entire Family

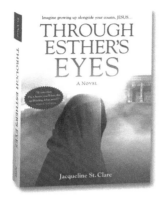

Through Esther's Eyes

The classic novel *The Red Tent* meets the acclaimed film *The Passion of the Christ* in this sweeping saga of the life of Jesus of Nazareth, as seen through the eyes of his fictional cousin, Esther. When Esther falls in love with Lazarus of Bethany, she thinks that her role as a woman will be complete with their marriage and children. Hidden in the action of the plot is an experience for all women to discover their true purpose and worth, modeled after Esther's wise "aunt," the Blessed Virgin Mary. You may know how the story ends, but you will be enthralled by seeing the power and the glory unfold anew in this remarkable first novel. Paperback. 464 pages. Y110-TEBK

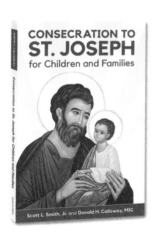

Consecration to St. Joseph for Children and Families

By Scott L. Smith, Jr. and Fr. Donald H. Calloway, MIC

Protect your family! Entrust your family to St. Joseph. Why? Because God, Himself, did. God entrusted the Holy Family to St. Joseph to keep them safe, and so should you. Drawing on the wealth of the Church's living tradition, Fr. Donald Calloway, MIC and Scott L. Smith, Jr., call on all of us to turn to St. Joseph, entrust ourselves, our children and families, our Church, and our world to our spiritual father's loving care. Watch for wonders when the Universal Patron of the Church opens the floodgates of Heaven to pour out graces into your family's lives. Paperback. 160 pages. Y110-CJHB

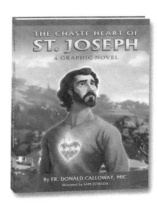

The Chaste Heart of Joseph
A Graphic Novel

How much do you really know about St. Joseph? He was once a little boy and played like all children. He had royal blood, and could have been a king. He was a young man when he married Mary. He was the brave and steadfast protector of the Holy Family. He's the model of manhood … and he had a pure, chaste heart. Join Fr. Donald Calloway, MIC, as he tells the dynamic and inspiring story of St. Joseph, our spiritual father and the "Terror of Demons," in this unique graphic novel for all ages, illustrated by Sam Estrada. Hardcover. 84 pages. Y110-JOEG

Call 1-800-462-7426 or ShopMercy.org